I0114611

(32) N. M. Glatfelter M.D.

RECORD

OF

CASPER GLATTFELDER

OF

GLATTFELDEN,

CANTON ZURICH, SWITZERLAND,

IMMIGRANT, 1743,

AND OF

HIS DESCENDANTS,

IN PART, COMPRISING 861 FAMILIES.

COMPILED BY

NOAH MILLER GLATFELTER, M. D.,

ST. LOUIS, MO.

1901.

ST. LOUIS:
NIXON-JONES PRINTING CO.
1901.

Notice

In many older books, foxing (or discoloration) occurs and, in some instances, print lightens with wear and age. Reprinted books, such as this, often duplicate these flaws, notwithstanding efforts to reduce or eliminate them. The pages of this reprint have been digitally enhanced and, where possible, the flaws eliminated in order to provide clarity of content and a pleasant reading experience.

Record of Casper Glattfelder of Glattfelden, Canton Zurich, Switzerland, Immigrant, 1743, and of His Descendants, In Part, Comprising 861 Families

Copyright © 1901 Noah Miller Glatfelter, M. D.

Originally published
St. Louis, MO.
1901

Reprinted by:

Janaway Publishing, Inc.
732 Kelsey Ct.
Santa Maria, California 93454
(805) 925-1038
www.janawaygenealogy.com

2014

ISBN: 978-1-59641-336-8

Made in the United States of America

DEDICATION.

TO THE WORTHY DEAD; TO THE MANY KIND FRIENDS WHO
HAVE MANIFESTED THEIR INTEREST IN THIS WORK,
THIS HISTORY OF THE GLATFELTER FAMILY
IS SINCERELY DEDICATED.

NOAH M. GLATFELTER, M. D.

CONTENTS.

| 2nd. | 3rd. Gen. | 4th Gen. | 4th Gen |

Casper

JOHN.

John, George
- Rebecca=Elicker.
- John.
- Moses.
- George. — Jacob. Peter. John. George. Jonathan. Cornelius. Dinah=Krout. Leah.d.young.
- Mary=Rule.
- Catharine=Weirman.
- Lydia=Walker.
- Solomon.
- Elizabeth-Lentz.

Susan-Forscht, Jacob
- Daniel.
- Jacob.
- Isaac. — Henry. Sarah. Samuel. Elizabeth=Miller. Zachariah. Susanna. Israel. Maria.
- Jesse.
- Elizabeth=Keesey.
- Mary=Bupp.
- Sarah=Simmons.
- Catharine=Werner.
- Lucinda=Holland.

Rosanna-Ferree, Eva=Raver
- Jacob.
- Samuel. — Israel. Henry. Susanna=Dellinger. Andrew. John. Eliza-Druck. Samuel. Lydia=Dietz.
- Catharine=Glatfelter.
- Eva.
- Magdalena-Walter.
- Lydia=Snyder.
- John.
- Manasses.

Daniel. — Jacob. Samuel. Daniel. Elija. Susan. Elizabeth.

Catharine Unm.

HENRY.

Michael.
- Caroline-Lepo.
- Ephraim B.
- Sarah-Emig.
- Matilda=Krout.
— Henry B. Jacob B. Andrew. Rudy. David B.

Jacob.
- Henry K.
- John.
— Leah=Moyer. Michael d. young. Mary. George. Hezekiah. Cordelia=Klinedinst. Louisa Un. m. Lavina d. young.

Daniel.
- Daniel.
- Sarah=Folcomer.
- Eliza-1-Fischel-2 Wolf.
- Melvina=Eyster.

Philip to Juniata Co.
- Susan=Flamer.2=Moyer.
- Rebecca-Miller.
- Mattie.
- Leah d. young.

Harry, Amelia=Hosler.
- Jacob d. young.
- Harry d. young.
- Catharine.
— Daniel. John. Adam. Jacob. Catharine=Myers.

Frederick.
- Solomon to Ohio.
- Daughter to Baltimore.
— Eva=Miller. Nancy=Bowers.

Genealogy to 4th. Gen.

CASPER.

- ROSANNA = BOYER.
- JOHN. — — —
  - ISAAC K.
  - JOHN.
  - SAMUEL.
  - JULIANN = SCHWER.
- CASPER. — — —
  - JACOB. — — — —
    - JACOB S.
    - FREDERICK. to ILLINOIS.
    - CASPER. to KANSAS.
    - GEORGE. to ILLINOIS.
    - JOHN. to OHIO.
    - DAVID. to ILLINOIS.
    - MAGDALENA. = FORSCHT.
    - SUSAN = TARBOX.
    - NANA = HACK.
    - CLARA.
- ADAM.
  - JESSE.
  - ELIZABETH = PITTENGER.
- JACOB. to CLINTON Co.
  - MARY = KETTNER.
- EVA d. young.
  - LYDIA = HENDERSON
  - SARAH = KESTER.
- JOSEPH. — — — ?
  - LEVI in KANSAS. — — — { JOSEPH. d. unm
- CHARLES to IND.

MICHAEL { GEORGE to OHIO. {
- A SON.
- A DAUGHTER.

Casper. — **FELIX.**

- CASPER to OHIO. — — —
  - WILLIAM to IOWA.
  - CHARLES to MO.
  - J. PETER.
  - LEAH, RACHEL, KATY.
    - LEAH = FALKENSTINE.
    - JONAS.
    - CHARLES.
    - MARY d. at 19.
    - JACOB d. at 17.
- PHILIP. — — — —
  - PHILIP G. — — — —
  - BENJAMIN.
  - NANCY = KOOP.
  - SUSAN = GRONE.
  - GEORGE.
    - PHILIP.
    - JESSE.
    - LYDIA = DIEHL.
    - CATHARINE = FOLCKOMER.
    - REBECCA = M. GENTZLER.
    - ELIZABETH = WAGNER.
- DANIEL. — — — {
  - DALLAS.
  - EMANUEL.
- JACOB to TENN.
  - ISRAEL to OHIO.
  - CHARLES.
  - BARBARA = GISE.
  - ELIZA = BAHN.
    - JACOB.
    - FREDERICK to ILL.
    - JOSEPH to ILL.
    - JOHN.
    - SAMUEL to LANC. Co.
- JOHN. — — — —
  - MARGARET = STAUFFER.
    - DANIEL. J.
    - BARBARA.
    - SARAH = NEFF.
    - ELIZABETH = GENTZLER.
    - MARY = J GENTZLER.
- FREDERICK. — — {
  - GRANVILLE.
  - DIETRICH.
  - ANNA M. = FAHS.
- MARGARET = FOLCKOMER {
- BARBARA = HOVIS. —
  - HENRY.
  - JACOB.
  - BARBARA = FILBEY.
  - MAGARETTE = LOWE.
  - WILLIAM to IND.
  - JOHATHAN to OHIO.
  - ELIZABETH = SECHRIST.
  - JOHN to OHIO. — —
  - DANIEL to JUNIATA Co.
  - CHARLES to OHIO.
  - MARY to OHIO.
    - DANIEL.
    - CATHARINE = MARKLE.
    - RACHEL = HESS.
    - ISAAC.
    - JACOB.
    - ELIZABETH = SHAFFER.
    - JESSE.
    - ADAM.
    - FRANKLIN.
- ELIZABETH = HARTMAN — — — — — { RACHEL, REBECCA, BARBARA

Genealogy to 4th. Gen.

PREFACE.

Jonathan Glatfelter, father of the author of this volume, was born in the year 1803, and reared in Springfield Township, York County, Pa., being the region where Casper Glatfelter, the original immigrant, settled, the center from which all the various branches radiated. Being, therefore, most favorably situated for obtaining a knowledge of the spreading of the family, and being endowed with a good memory, active and intelligent faculties, it is to him we are indebted for the possibility enabling us, at this late day, to unravel the early branchings of the parent stem. On April 30, 1859, the author, then 21 years of age, constructed a family tree from his father's dictation, placing every then known name in proper relation. With this manuscript tree still in his possession, he has been enabled to place every living descendant of whom he has knowledge to his proper niche, as he believes, on the Great Family Tree. Without this document, the writer does not hesitate to state, the accomplishment of this work would, to-day, be an utter impossibility. Records of our early ancestors are very limited — inscriptions on tombstones, often obliterated, traditions confused and mostly unreliable. Being in possession, therefore, of the only key wherewith to unlock the past, the author felt an incumbent responsibility which would not be shaken off. He was impressed with the idea that it was a good work that *ought* to be done; and, though now unappreciated by some, the encouragement received from others, together with the conviction that as the years roll by the importance of his work will be more and more realized, became a sufficient motive to engage in it. A work of this kind must be a labor of love. Financial considerations, even if ample, which is seldom the case, are no adequate recompense.

1

Owing to the strenuous pressure of our daily necessities, we are too apt to forget our noble forefathers, who, impelled by the love of civic and religious liberty, braved the hardships of pioneer life, and by infinite sacrifices paved the way for us. We should cherish their memories and venerate them with pious remembrance. Even heathen nations outdo us in pious homage of their ancestors. The sentiment of patriotism must have its beginning in sentiment of family, and they whose sympathies are bounded by their own narrow circle of near relatives, are not likely to be imbued with those higher spiritual inculcations of neighborliness to all men. Moreover, being careless of their origin, they are likely to be likewise careless of their destiny.

The author is indebted to many friends for generous help. Among those deserving special mention, are Mr. Luther Glatfelter, Rev. Adam Stump, both of York, Pa.; Lewis K. Glatfelter, of Neiman, Pa.; Mr. James Glatfelter, Mount Joy, Pa., and, above all, to Mr. Granville Glatfelter, Brillhart Station, Pa., who was untiring in aiding to make the record complete. The work is submitted to the generous consideration of my friends, believing it will fulfill all reasonable expectations. Inaccuracies and omissions no doubt occur. Only those who undertake similar work can realize the extent of labor demanded. The author requests to be informed of all mistakes and omissions, to the end that should a second edition be called for, either he or some other may make the corrections. He regrets exceedingly that the limits of his book did not permit of fuller personal narratives, which, in many cases, are very interesting.

NOAH M. GLATFELTER, M. D.

HISTORICAL.

"The Rhenish Palatinate and places adjacent have furnished the ancestors of those citizens of York Co., who now constitute its principal families in wealth and culture." * The emigration was very extensive from 1727 to 1750–1760. They came down the Rhine, took ship at the seaport, Rotterdam and landed at Philadelphia. We are in possession of the registers of the various ship-loads of emigrants arriving there, now published in the Pennsylvania archives, Vol. 17, 2d series, 1890. Among the passengers of the good ship "Francis and Elizabeth," was "Gasper Gladfelder," aged 33 years, who with the rest *qualified* August 30th, 1743. He came from Glattfelden, Canton Zurich, Switzerland. The evidence is as follows: First, Casper Glattfelder, son of Felix Glattfelder and Barbara Gorius, was baptized 1709. See old church record of the town of Glattfelden, investigated by Mr. Edwin Jaggli, of same place, in behalf of my friend S. F. Glatfelter, York, Pa.

Second. "Casper Glattfelder and family, together with many other families and persons, emigrated to North America, 1743." This record is taken from a little book, a "History of the Glattfelden Church," by A. Nef, issued 1863, at Bülach, Ct. Zurich, and reported to me by the well-known historian of Switzerland, Prof. Dr. Dändliker of Zurich. The same writes to me, he has no doubt whatever that all bearing the name Glattfelder had their orgin at Glattfelden, which name is derived from "Feld der Glatt," a branch of the Rhine river. Also, that at various places throughout the Canton of Zurich the name is still to be met with. So then, these records established: 1709, baptized; 33 years old; 1743,

---

* See Hist. York Co., 1886. — Gibson.

landed. The only Glattfelder on record having entered the State of Pennsylvania, makes the inference conclusive that this Casper was our great ancestor. Glattfelder, it seems, should be the spelling.

Very recently, after the foregoing was written, the author received a letter in answer to one of inquiry from Mr. Henry Glattfelder, residing at Indianapolis, Ind., confirmatory of the Swiss orgin of the Glatfelter family. This Henry was born 1849, in Bezirk (Section) Bülach, Ct. Zurich. He has a brother, John, living at Baden, Ct. Aargau; also a sister married to R. Shellenberger, whose son, Mr. R. Shellenberger, at Indianapolis, a more recent immigrant, was the means of the above communication. Attention is directed to what, no doubt, was the original orthography of the name, probably dating back to the time when that region was first occupied by a German tribe.

Casper Glatfelter settled in Springfield township, York county. At that period the town of York was but two years old; only 23 lots had been taken, and no more until 1746. The county was part of Lancaster county until 1749. As regards the orthography of the name, it is to be noted that the registered form was by the ship's officers, phonetically. The same applies to the spelling we find in the muster rolls of the Revolutionary soldiers enrolled in the county of York, where we come across the names of four of the sons of Casper. "Casper Clotfelter" is enrolled in the 5th Company, Capt. John Erman, 7th Battalion, Col. David Kennedy. In the 6th Company, Capt. George Geiselman, we find Henry, Michael and Felix "Klotfelter" enrolled.* At the present day I find the spelling also "Glattfelder," "Clodfelter," "Gladfelter," "Clotfelter" and "Clotfelder." Finally, in one branch, the name has changed to "Glotfelty." The author begs pardon if, in the body of his work, he occasionally misplaces a *d* or a *t* in spelling the name. Such mistakes were unavoidable.

---

* See "The Spangler Families," by Edw. W. B. Spangler, York, Pa., 1896.

TWO OTHER IMMIGRANTS.

Very recently there came to the writer's knowledge the names of two immigrants from Europe, constituting two entirely distinct branches of the Glattfelder family. One of them landed at Baltimore, the other at a seaport of North Carolina. The name of the first was Solomon Clotfelder, born 1738, arrived 1765, settling near Grantsville, Md., 1766, then in 1795 moved to Salisbury, Somerset county, Pa., where he died, 1818, in his 81st year. He was the father of nine children, four sons and five daughters. Jacob, the youngest, was born 1784. Jacob had six sons and two daughters. One, named Michael, moved to Fairfield, Iowa. The youngest son, John, had nine children, seven sons and two daughters. One of the sons was killed in the Civil War. One, named Josiah M., to whose kindly favor I am indebted for these facts, moved to Lanark, Ill., 1864. A member of the board of education, evidences his standing in his community. He has two sons, aged 20 and 33. Read backward we have, therefore, the sons[5] of Josiah M.[4], of John[3], of Jacob[2], of Solomon[1]. A published sketch of this branch of the family, respecting the descendants of the original Solomon, evidences their excellent character and honorable standing in the communities where residing. The author regrets that the plan of his book could not also include a full record of this very numerous family; he, however, begs to extend the hand of friendly greeting to it. The name has undergone a singular change, being now written *Glotfelty*. When this change took place appears not known to the present generation.

For an account of the other branch mentioned above, the writer is indebted to Doctor George A. Clotfelter, of Hillsboro, Ill. His great-great-grandfather, named George, lived in North Carolina. Whether an immigrant, is not now certainly known, but at least probable. His speech was German. He had a large family. One son, David, on his way westward, died in the mountains of Tennessee (1833). His widow, five sons and two daughters continued the journey to Cape Girardeau, Mo., leaving after a few months and settling in Montgomery County, Ill.   One of these sons, named George L., had a son named David H., who is the father of Dr. George A., my informant.   "There is in the county a small army of relations," he says.   One son of the original George, named Philip, settled in Perry, or Cape Girardeau county, Mo., where his descendants are now resident.   They write their name Clodfelter.   How interesting if the three branches could be traced back to the same household, perhaps!

PLAN OF ARRANGEMENT.

Casper Glattfelder, the immigrant stem, as already stated, located in Springfield township, probably at or near Glatfelter Station, Pa. R. R.   He was the father of five sons, named Felix, Henry, Michael, Casper, and John, no daughters.   The first four were soldiers of the Revolution.   John is not on record as a soldier.   We obtain an historical glimpse of four of the sons in 1783.   In the list of taxables of N. Codorus township, we find the names of Felix and Michael, and of Shrewsbury township (part of which later became Springfield township), the names of John for 240 acres, and of Henry for 146 acres.*

Michael had an only son, George, who moved to Ohio and had son and daughter.   Here our knowledge of this branch ends.   Our account, therefore, will be limited to the remaining four sons, or branches, naturally forming four grand divisions or parts of the body of this work.   The order of birth is not known, neither of these sons nor their children.   The third generation will be divided into chapters, as follows: —

---

* See History York county, 1886. — Gibson.

Part I. — John.

Chapt. 1st, John.
" 2d, George.
" 3d, Daniel.
" 4th, Jacob.

Chapt. 5th, Susan = Forscht.
" 6th, Eva = Raver.
" 7th, Rosanna = Ferree.

Part II. — Felix.

Chapt. 8th, Daniel.
" 9th, Philip.
" 10th, John.
" 11th, Frederick.

Chapt. 12th, Barbara = Hovis.
" 13th, Margaretta = Folckommer.
" 14th, Casper.

Part III. — Casper.

Chapt. 15th, John.
" 16th, Casper.

Chapt. 17th, Jacob.

Part IV. — Henry.

Chapt. 18th, Michael.
" 19th, Jacob.

Chapt. 20th, Daniel.
" 21st, Harry.

EXPLANATORY.

The families only are numbered. The system, though simple, will be found practically efficient. The figures above the names indicate the generations; thus, figure 5 above a name means belonging to the 5th generation. Abbreviations used: b., born; d., dead or died; m. or =, married; unm., unmarried; res., residing or resided; ch., children; lab., laborer; farm., farmer; Luth., adheres to Lutheran church; Ref., to Reformed church; Presb., to Presbyterian church; U. B., to United Brethren; U. Evang., to United Evangelical; Episc., Episcopal church; Meth., Methodist Episcopal; unaf., unaffiliated, not joined any church; un., unknown; cig. mnf., cigar manufacturer; c. m., or cig. m., cigar maker; pref., preference.

Two indexes are supplied for family names, one for the Glatfelters, one for all others connected.

CASPER¹ GLATTFELDER (Sen.), immigrant, b. 1709 at Glattfelden, Canton Zurich, Switzerland. He had 5 sons: (2) John; (283) Felix; (631) Casper; (685b) Henry; Michael (see p. 6).

PART I. — JOHN², AND DESCENDANTS.

2.

JOHN² GLATFELTER (Casper¹) res. Springfield twp., York co., Pa. Ch.:

(3) John, b. 1778, d. 1821.   (230) Susan, 1794–1868.
(91) George, b. 1788, d. 1868. (240) Eva, d. 1852.
(107) Daniel.   (259) Rosanna
(128) Jacob.   Catharine d. young.

CHAPTER 1ST. — JOHN³.

3.

JOHN³ GLATFELTER (John², Casper¹), m. Dorothy Walter who d. 1851, aged 71 yrs. He was a farmer, res. Springfield twp., both buried at the "White" church. Ch.: (4) Peter; (12) Jonathan, 1803–1883; (50) John, 1804–1889; (64) Jacob, 1813–1880; (74) George; (86) Dinah; Cornelius and Leah, both d. young.

4.

PETER[4] GLATFELTER (John[3], John[2], &c.), m. Catharine Raver. Farm. near Loganville, Pa. Ch.: (5) Priscilla, 1839; Solomon, unm.; (9) Absalom; (11) Angelina, 1875; Mary, unm.; (10) Jacob; Peter, 1840, unm., res. Lanc. co., Pa. Solomon was a soldier in the civil war, d. aged 62.

5.

Priscilla[5] Glatfelter (Peter[4], John[3], &c.), m. Mr. Henn, retired farmer, res. Belmont, Iowa. U. Evang. Ch.: (6) Geo. W.; (7) Catharine E.; (8) Emmeline; (10) Jacob, unm.

6.

George[6] W. Henn (Priscilla[5], Peter[4], &c.), m. Rose Jansen, daughter of a minister of the Ref. church. Farmer, res. at Lake Beton, Lincoln co., Minn. Ch.: Lydia, 1890; Paul W., 1892; William, 1894; Aaron, 1896; John, 1898; baby, 1900.

7.

Catharine[6] E. Henn (Priscilla[5], &c.), m. John L. Pals, farm. res. at Merservey, Franklin co., Iowa. Ch.: Larmert, 1889; Priscilla, 1890; Alocha, 1892; Catharine, 1894; John, 1896; Emmeline, 1898; Richard, 1899; baby, 1900.

8.

Emmeline[6] Henn (Priscilla[5], &c.), m. Geo. A. Ell, mason, res. Klemme, Hancock co., Iowa. Twelve years married. Ch. 0.

9.

Absalom[5] Glatfelter (Peter[4], John[3], &c.), m. Dinah Lentz. Ch.: 12. Res. given at Columbia Grove, Iowa, but not found.

10.

Jacob[5] Glatfelter (Peter[4], &c.), m. Ella Strickler. Res. at Campbell Sta., York co., Pa. Ch.: One.

11.

Angelina Glatfelter (Peter[4], &c.), m. Joseph Peters, who died
    1882. The widow lives at York with a sister, they
    together owning a farm near York.

12.

(12) JONATHAN[4] GLATFELTER (John[3], John[2], &c.), m.
    Elizabeth Miller, b. 1808, d. 1885. A cooper by trade, turned
    to farming and reared his family near Yost's mill, York
    twp. When the children were grown, and had mostly
    scattered, he moved to Loganville. He was an adherent
    of the Reformed church. He was the historian, without
    whom an account of the relationship of the Galtfelters
    would have been an impossibility, and the book could
    not have been compiled. Ch.:

Cornelius, d. young.	Maria, d. at 4 years.
(13) Matilda, 1832.	(38) Eliza.
(22) Israel, 1835.	(42) Caroline, 1845.
(27) William, 1836.	(44) Jonathan M., 1843.
(32) Noah M., 1837.	(47) Leo, 1848.
(33) Sarah, 1839.	(48) John M., 1850.

13.

(13) Matilda[5] Glatfelter (Jonathan[4], &c.), m. Geo. Living-
    ston, farm. res. near Strinestown, Pa. Luth. Ch.:

(14) Ellen, 1854.	(18) Jacob, 1861.
(15) Reuben, 1857.	(19) Lizzie, 1863.
Sarah, 1859–1862.	(20) Leo, 1872.
(17) George F., 1862	(21) Tillie, 1868.
Minnie, 1874–1874.	Albert, unm., 1877.

14.

(14) Ellen[6] Livingston (Matilda[5], Jonathan[4], &c.), m.
    Joseph Harman. Dealer in carriages, Wellsville, Pa.
    Meth. Ch.: One, Roy, b. 1880, a public school
    teacher.

(12) JONATHAN GLATFELTER.

15.

Reuben[6] Livingston (Matilda[5], &c.), m. Elizabeth Fickes. Trade is milling. Res. N. York, Pa. Luth. Ch.:
(16) Cora E., 1877.   Fannie G., 1887.
     Howard O., 1879.   Elsie R., 1889.

16.

Cora[7] E. Livingston (Reuben[6], Matilda[5], &c.), m. Harvey A. Jacobi, c. mnf. N. York.

17.

George[6] F. Livingston (Matilda[5], &c.), m. Annie Dietz. Salesman. Luth. Res. Yorkana, Pa. Ch.: Saidie, 1892; Roy L., 1894; Geo. F., 1891–1892; Stuard H., 1898.

18.

Jacob[6] G. Livingston (Matilda[5], &c.), m. Ida Martin. A miller by trade, now in the livery and boarding stable business. York, Pa. Unaf. Ch.: Tremen L., 1887–1893; Jacob N., 1889; Mabel F., 1891; Geo. M., 1894; Margarete, 1899.

19.

Lizzie[6] Livingston (Matilda[5], &c.), m. David Seip. Farm. Res. Zion's View, York co. Ch.: One son, Kerwin.

20.

Leo[6] G. Livingston (Matilda[5], &c.,) m. Amanda Kauffman. Shipping clerk. Luth. Res. N. York. Ch.: One dght. Grace R., 1899.

21.

Tillie[6] Livingston (Matilda[5], &c.), m. first to Chas. Allison; 2d to Calvin F. Fetrow. Res. York, Pa. Luth. Ch.: Lester E. (Fetrow), 1889; Laura (Fetrow), 1891.

22.

Israel[5] Glatfelter (Jonathan[4], John[3], &c.), m. first, Rebecca Emig. Ch.: 10 ; 2d to Mrs. Kate (Emig) Hyde, a sister. Ch. 0. Trade is tailoring, but engaged in a general mercantile business, to which he added milling and farming. Known for indomitable perseverance and push. Res. Glen Rock, Pa. Luth. Ch. :

Richard F., 1860–1881.   John F., 1871, unm.

Penrose E., 1862, unm.   (26) James A., 1873.

(23) Robert, 1864.   Sallie E., 1876, unm.

(24) Harvey, 1866.   Annie R., 1878, unm.

(25) Wiltie, 1867–1898.   Abdon, 1880.

23.

Robert[6] Glatfelter (Israel[5], Jonathan[4], &c.), m. Emma Meckley. Merchant tailor. Res. Glen Rock, Pa. Preference, Evang. Ch.:

Florence, 1890.   Robert, 1893–1900.

Nora, 1892.   Harry, 1896.

24.

Harvey[6] Glatfelter (Israel[5], &c.), m. Clara Lichtenberger. Res. Manchester, Pa. Proprietor of marble works. Unaf. Ch. : Oscar L., 1891; Jesse V., 1893; Clark W., 1895 ; Edgar, 1897; Mary M., 1899.

25.

Wiltie[6] Glatfelter (Israel[5], &c.), m. Clara Lentz. Superintended his father's mill at Glen Rock, Luth. Ch.: Myrtle R., 1891 ; Claude M., 1893; Neva R., 1895; May E., 1897–1898 ; Wiltie I., 1898.

26.

James[6] A. Glatfelter (Israel[5], &c.)., m. Mamie Rentzel. Proprietor marble works, Mt. Joy, Lanc. co., Pa. U. B. Ch.: 0.

27.

William⁵ Glatfelter (Jonathan⁴, John³, &c.), m. first Catharine Flinchbaugh; second, Elizabeth Leader. Carpenter and retired farmer. Now a pensioned soldier of the Civil War. Res. Yoe, Pa. Without denominational bias he is a leader in the "Church of God." Ch.:

Mary A., 1858–1860;   (30) Elizabeth, 1869.
(28) Wilson G., 1860;   (31) Noah, 1872.
(29) Ida, 1867.

28.

Wilson⁶ Glatfelter (William⁵, Jonathan⁴, &c.), m. Lizzie E. Hess. Dealer in furniture, &c., Dallastown, Pa. U. B. Ch.: Beulah M., 1886–1886; Raymond, 1888–1889; Esther O., 1893.

29.

Ida⁶ Glatfelter (William⁵, &c.), m. Samuel Raver, blacksmith. Res. Hopewell twp., Rye P. O. "Church of God." Ch.: Washington, 1885–1888; Laura B., 1887; Samuel M., 1888; Milton B., 1896; Ralph, 1899–1900.

30.

Elizabeth⁶ E. Glatfelter (William⁵, &c.), m. Michael Dellinger. Farm. Hopewell twp. Unaf. Ch.: Minnie E., 1892; Mamie E., 1894; John H., 1896; Nora M., 1898; Norman C., 1900.

31.

Noah⁶ Glatfelter (William, &c.), m. to ——. Res. Yoe, Pa. Ch.: 0.

32.

Noah⁵ M. Glatfelter, M. D. (Jonathan⁴, John³, &c.), m. Mary Hegarty of Philadelphia. Graduated Doctor of Medicine from the University of Pennsylvania, 1864; served as Asst. Surg. U. S. Vols., commissioned by the President, and was mustered out 1867. He then located in and near St. Louis practicing his profession since. In early life united with the Reformed church, but is not now affiliated. Ch.: Lisbeth M., 1869; Florence M., 1875, d. 1893; Edith E., 1877; Alice M. M., 1880; Herbert S., 1882; Grace A., 1884, d. 1892; Eva E., 1886, d. 1892.

33.

Sarah[5] Glatfelter (Jonathan[4], &c.), m. Samuel Williams, farm. York twp. Unaf. Ch.:

(34) Clara, 1868.   (37) Sallie, 1874.
(35) Minnie E., 1871.   Samuel, 1881.
(36) Maggie, 1873.

34.

Clara[6] Williams (Sarah,[5] Jonathan,[4] &c.), m. Charles A. Reilly, timekeeper coal & iron co. Res. Pottstown, Pa. Unaf. Ch.: Theresa, 2 yrs. old; Paul, 1 yr.

35.

Minnie[6] E. Williams (Sarah,[5] &c.), m. William Austine, teacher and bookkeeper. Res. Yoe, Pa. Ch.: Carl T., 1893; Melba, 1895; Eva, 1899.

36.

Maggie[6] Williams (Sarah[5], &c.), m. Elmer Tyson; business, general merchandise, Red Lion, Pa. Unaf. Ch.: 0.

37.

Sallie[6] Williams (Sarah[5], &c.), m. Jesse Erhart, teacher. Res. Dallastown, Pa. Pref. Luth. Unaf. Ch.: Alma L., 1899.

38.

Eliza[5] Glatfelter (Jonathan[4], John[3], &c.), m. Peter T. Goodling, retired farm. Res. Loganville, Pa. Luth. Wife dead about 20 yrs. Ch.:

(39) William H., 1864.   John R., 1872, d. young.
(40) Andrew J., 1866.   Ida S., 1874-1900.
(41) Jacob F., 1867.

39.

William[6] H. Goodling (Eliza[5], Jonathan[4], &c.), m. Rebecca Sheffer. Farm., at the old homestead, Potosi, Pa. Luth. Ch.: Elsie M., 1896; Beulah, 1899.

40.

James[6] A. Goodling (Eliza[5], &c.), m. Susan Erhart. Farm. Res. near Glen Rock, Pa. Luth. Ch.: Allen C., 1887; Edna E., 1889; Kerwin S., 1893; Belle V., 1895; Howard L., 1898.

41.

Jacob[6] F. Goodling (Eliza[5], &c.), Ella O. Smith. Teacher, and agt. Phosphate Co. Res. Loganville, Pa. Luth. Ch.: Clark O., 1892; Marie N., 1894.

42.

Caroline[5] Glatfelter (Jonathan[4], John[3], &c.), m. Spangler Hildebrand, carpenter and farm. Res. Loganville, Pa. Luth. Ch. (43): Curtis, 1871; Beulah, 1883.

43.

Curtis[6] Hildebrand (Caroline[5], Jonathan[4], &c.), m. Martha L. Yost. Teacher of music. Res. York, Pa. Ref. Ch.: One, Perry C., 1899.

44.

Jonathan[5] M. Glatfelter (Jonathan[4], John[3], &c.), m. Emma E. Sheffer. Teacher and merchant, also justice of the peace; wounded in the Civil War, is now a pensioned veteran. Luth. Ch.: Elma J., 1866-1868; Jennie L., 1869-1872; (45) James A., 1871; (46) Homer L., 1875; Annie K., 1878; Agnes I., 1880; William E., 1883; Gerald J., 1887.

45.

James[6] A. Glatfelter (Jonathan[5], &c.), m. Mamie Garver. Office clerk. Res. Phila., Pa. Unaf. Ch.: James P., 1898; Marie, 1897, died; Emily, infant.

46.

Homer[6] L. Glatfelter (Jonathan[5], &c.), m. Mardie Minichan. Salesman. Harrisburg, Pa. Pref. Luth. Ch.: Sarah E., 1897; Samuel J., 1898; Horace, 1899.

47.

Leo[5] Glatfelter (Jonathan[4], John[3], &c.), m. Clementine M. Bair. General merchandise and fruit-growing. Res. Loganville. Pref. Luth. A pensioned soldier. Ch.: Nimrel, 1872; Howard, 1873; Cornelius L., 1875; Erma, 1876; Charles H., 1880; Laura E., 1882; Walter S., 1890.

48.

John[5] M. Glatfelter (Jonathan[4], John[3], &c.), m. Sarah Plymeyer. Wagoner, farm., and Ins. Ag't. Unaf. Res. Loganville, Pa. Ch.: (49) J. Monroe, Oct. 8, 1869; William H., 1871; Carrie E., 1873, d. inf.

49.

J. Monroe[6] Glatfelter (John[5] M., Jonathan[4], &c.), m. Clara M. Sheffer. Paper hanger. Loganville, Pa. Unaf. Ch.: Edwood H., 1892; Annetta J., 1897; Arthur J., 1899.

50.

JOHN[4] GLATFELTER (John[3], John[2], &c.), b. 1804, d. 1889; m. Susan Snyder. Farmer. Res. near Red Lion. Evang. Wife was born 1816, and now living with a daughter at Red Lion, Pa. Ch.:

(51) Henry, 1841.   (56) Leo.
     Cornelius, d.   (57) Charles A., 1866–1896.
(52) Samuel S., 1844.   (58) William S., 1851.
(54) John, 1846.   (59) Sarah A., 1846.
     Pius, unm.   (62) Nelson, 1860.
(55) Emanuel.   (63) Lydiann.

51.

Henry[5] Glatfelter (John[4], John[3], &c.). Stone building contractor. Mansfield, Ohio. Luth. Ch.: Dora E., 1870; Estella M., 1874–1875; Franklin W., 1876–1886; Elmer C., 1880; Olive F., 1889–1890; Helen E., 1891.

52.

Samuel[5] S. Gladfelter (John[4], &c.), m. Susan Grim. Farm and cig. mnf. Hartley, Pa. U. Evang. Ch.: T. M., 1872, teacher; (53) Jennie M., 1875; Minnie L., 1877; Hattie V., 1880; James B., 1884, d. inf.

53.

Jennie[6] M. Gladfelter (Samuel[5] S., John[4], &c.), m. James E. Diehl, farm. Luth. Ch.: Irvine P., 1895; Harvey L., 1897; Irene, 1898.

54.

John[5] S. Gladfelter (John[4], &c.), m. Mary Sechrist. Farm. Res. near Yoe, Pa. U. B. Ch.: Clarence A., 1881; John C., 1883; Virgie E., 1885; Purdie A., 1888; Adam F., 1891; Jennie A., 1894–1895.

55.

Emanuel[5] Gladfelter (John[4], &c.), m. Agnes Snyder; farm. Winterstown, Pa. Unaf. Ch.: Augusta and Howard.

56.

Leo[5] Gladfelter (John[4], &c.), m. Amanda E——. Carpenter and painter. Yorkana, Pa. Unaf. Ch.: Kerwin H., 1885; Gertie E., 1891; Earl G., 1895.

57.

Charles[5] A. Glatfelter (John[4], &c.), m. Alice R. Miller. Cig. m. and painter. Red Lion. U. B. Ch.: One, Harry A., 1893.

58.

William[5] S. Gladfelter (John[4], &c.), m. Sarah Grim. Cig. mnf. Felton, Pa. U. B. Ch.: Cora E., 1880–1885; Alice E., 1881; Charles, 1883; James, 1885; Anna, 1888–1890; Ralph, 1891, d. inf.; Irwin, 1893.

59.

Sarah A. Gladfelter (John[4], &c.), m. Henry Grim, lab. R. R. Red Lion. U. B. Ch.: (60) Pius March 5, 1874; Emma, 1876; Ida, 1877; (61) Sadie, 1874; Charles, 1883–1895.

60.

Pius[6] Grim (Sarah[5] A., John[4], &c.), m. Ida S. Flinchbaugh. Cig. m. Unaf. Res. Red Lion. Ch.: One, Walter L., 1898.

61.

Sadie[6] Grim (Sarah[5] A., John[4], &c.), m. Bert C. Smith, cig. shipper. Red Lion. U. B. Ch.: Robert R., 1897; Nora, 1899.

62.

Nelson[5] Glatfelter (John[4], &c.), m. Minnie Myers. Painter. Red Lion. Unaf. Ch.: One, Roy M., 1898–1899.

63.

Lydiann[5] Gladfelter (John[4], &c.), m. John W. Strayer, cig. mnf. Red Lion. U. B. Ch.: James F., 1878; Emma M., 1880; John K., 1887.

64.

JACOB[4] GLATFELTER (John[3], &c.), m. Nancy Stover. Tailor and farm. Loganville, Pa. An elder, many years, (Luth.) esteemed by all. Crossing a R. R. met a violent death. Ch.: Nathan, 1837, unm.; (71) Nancy, 1845; Alice, 1839, unm.; (73) Frances, 1852; (65) Amanda, 1841.

65.

Amanda[5] Glatfelter (Jacob[4], John[3], &c.), m. Elias Myers. Ch.: (66) Edward G., 1866; (69) Annie; (67) John H., 1862; (70) Charles G.; (68) Agnes; Harvey J., unm.

66.

Edward[6] G. Myers (Amanda[5], &c.), m. Emma[6] J. Glatfelter (of the branch Felix). Attorney at law. York, Pa., Luth. Ch.: Lulu B., 1888; Irene V., 1889.

67.

John[6] H. Myers (Amanda[5], &c.), m. Cornelia L. Weaver. Clothier and tailor. York, Pa. Luth. Ch.: Milfert W., 1890; Vesta A., 1885.

68.

Agnes[6] Myers (Amanda[5], &c.), m. W. T. Stover. Res. near Spring Grove. Ch.: Three.

69.

Annie[6] Myers (Amanda[5], &c.), m. Chas. W. Diehl (Rev.). Graduate Gettysburg Seminary. Ch.: One.

70.

Chas.[6] G. Myers (Amanda[5], &c.), m. to un. Farm. near Hanover Junction. Ch.: Three.

71.

Nancy[5] Glatfelter (Jacob[4], John[3], &c.), m. Edward Goodling, teacher. Res. Loganville, Pa. Luth. Ch.: Geo. E., 1870–1888; (72) Jennie K., 1874.

72.

Jennie[6] K. Goodling (Nancy[5], Jacob[4], &c.), m. Robert Goodling. Ch.: One, Geo. A., 1896.

73.

Frances[5] Glatfelter (Jacob[4], &c.), m. Urias Smith, cig. pck., Loganville. Ch.: Ellen O., 1872; Ida M., 1879–1880; William H., 1880; E. O., m. J. Goodling (see 41).

74.

GEORGE[4] GLATFELTER (John[3], John[2], &c.), m. Juliann
Lentz. Farm. near Loganville. Luth. Both d. Ch.:

(75) Cornelius L., 1846.   (81) Henry L.
(78) Albert L.   (83) Elenora L.
(80) Emanuel L., 1851.   (84) Jacob L., 1862.
(82) George L., 1852.   (85) John L.

Lydia, d. 1862.

75.

Cornelius[5] L. Glatfelter (George[4], &c.), m. Emeline Brenne-
man. Farm. near Loganville, Pa. Ref. Ch.: (76)
Albion, 1871; Lydiann, d. young; Edward, 1873–1875;
(77) Mary J., 1875; Franklin, 1879; Sevilla, 1877–1879;
Ida E., 1882; Louis H., 1884; Noah E., 1879; William
C., 1891.

76.

Albion[6] Glatfelter (Cornelius[5], George[4], &c.), m. Sadie Schell.
Res. Cedar Valley, Iowa. Ch.: 3.

77.

Mary[6] J. Glatfelter (Cornelius[5], &c.), m. Albert Devennie.
Res. Baltimore, Md. Ch.: One, Edith, 1899.

78.

Albert[5] L. Glatfelter (George[4], &c.), m. Sarah Klinedinst.
Lab. Res. Lebanon Pa. Luth. Ch.: (79) Orestus L.,
1868; Annie M., 1870; Joshua G., 1874; Ferda I., 1877,
Galertus E., 1882; Sallie L. E., 1887; inft. dght., d.
1889; Harry F., 1892. Joshua G. is m. Ch.: 0.

79.

Orestus[6] S. Glatfelter (Albert[5] L., George[4], &c.). Ch.: Dora
M., 1887; Annie N., Erestus F., Albert E., Sarah E.
Dewey H.

80.

Emanuel[5] Glatfelter (George[4], &c.), m. Jennie Klump. Carpenter. Cedar Rapids, Iowa. Unaf. Ch.: Archie K., 1879; John S., 1881; Paul V., 1890.

81.

Henry[5] L. Glatfelter (George[4], &c.), m. Annie Schultz: Res. Cedar Rapids, Iowa. Unaff. Ch.: Mary J., 1880; Henry E., 1887; Alice M., 1894.

82.

George[5] L. Glatfelter (George[4], &c.), m. Louisa Bachman. Physician, Iola, Kans. U. Evang. Ch.: Lucius B., 1876; George F., 1886.

83.

Elenora[5] L. Glatfelter (George[4], &c.), m. Amos. Bricker, farm. Seitzville, Pa. Ch.: 7.

84.

Jacob[5] L. Glatfelter (George[4], &c.), m. Frances Krout. Farm. near Loganville, Pa. Ref. Ch.: Mabel E., 1889; Joicy M., 1892; Paul S., 1894.

85.

John[5] L. Glatfelter (George[4], &c.), m. Emma Sheffer. Res. Cedar Valley, Iow. Ch.: 3.

86.

DINAH[4] GLATFELTER (John[3], John[2], &c.), m. William Krout, farm. Loganville, Pa. Luth. Both dead. Ch.: (87) John G.; (89) Alice, 1851.

87.

John[5] G. Krout (Dinah[4], John[3], &c.), m. un. Retired farm. Luth. Res. Loganville, Pa. Ch.: (88) Harry H., 1873; Ammon E., 1881–1883; Mamie J., 1885.

88.

Harry⁶ H. Krout (John⁵ G., Dinah⁴, &c.), m. Mollie Ness. Luth. Ch.: One, Raymond R., 1896.

89.

Alice⁵ Krout (Dinah⁴, &c.), m. Nelson Bricker, farm. Loganville. Lutheran. Husband d. Ch.: John H., 1879–1883; (90) Ida L. V., 1875; William H., 1880, d. inf.; Lloy S., 1884; Chas. A., 1890.

90.

Ida⁶ L. V. Bricker (Alice⁵, Dinah⁴, &c.), m. Adam Sweitzer. Ch.: 0.

Chapter 2nd. — GEORGE³.

91.

GEORGE³ GLATFELTER (John², Casper¹). Farmer. Res. Warrington twp., York co. Pa. Ch.:
(92) Rebecca; (93) John; (94) Moses; (95) Mary; (102) Lydia; (103) Solomon; (105) Elizabeth; George, d.; Catharine.

92.

REBECCA⁴ GLATFELTER (George³, John², &c.), m. John Elicker, Warrington, twp. Ch.: 5.

93.

JOHN⁴ GLATFELTER (George³, &c.), m. 1st, Kate Shelby. Ch.: One. 2d, Miss Kratzer. Ch.: 0.

94.

MOSES⁴ GLATFELTER (George³, &c.), b. 1816, d. 1891, m. Elizabeth Ruhl, who d. 1901, aet. 82 yrs. Res.

Warrington twp., Y. co. Pa. Ch.: 3; (94a) Christian R., 1841; (94d) Mary J., 1844; (94e) Wesley F., 1853; m. Sadie J. Martin. Ch.: Harry M., d. young; Blanche E., 1887, and George H., 1890.

94a.

Christian[5] R. Glatfelter (Moses[4], George[3], &c.), m. Annie E. Kutz. Ch.: 2; (94b) Sadie, m. George Albright. Ch.: 2; Preston, now 17 yrs., and inft. d. ; (94c) Willis E., m. Emma Bentline. Ch.: One, Ada, 6 yrs. old.

94d.

Mary[5] J. Glatfelter (Moses[4], &c.), m. 1st, B. D. Kutz ; m. 2d, J. B. Byres (d.).
All the above res. about $3\frac{1}{2}$ miles E. of Carlisle, Pa.

95.

MARY[4] GLATFELTER (George[3], &c.), m. Jesse Rule. Res. Cumberland co. Ch.: (96) George[5], m. Miss Wagner. Ch.: 2.
97. Obadiah[5], m. Miss Myers.
98. Jesse[5], m. Miss McCreary. Ch.: 3; (99) Christian[5], 1853; (100) Joseph[5], m. Miss Hertzler. Ch.: 2; (101) Catherine[5], m. John Strickler. Ch.: 2; Emma, d. unm.

99.

Christian[5] Rule (Mary[2], George[3], &c.), m. Elizabeth Kessler. A graduate of Dickinson College. Pa. An attorney at law since 1874. Res. Reading, Pa. Associated in his profession with the Hon. Daniel Ermentrout. Presby. Ch.: 0.

102.

LYDIA[4] GLATFELTER (George[3], &c.), m. Josiah Walker. Ch.: 5; Amanda, Jane, Rosie, Rilla, James, d. Res. Kassauqua, Iowa.

103.

SOLOMON[4] GLATFELTER (George[3], &c.), b. Nov. 21, 1828, m. Sarah A. Bentz. Farm. Rossville, Pa. Formerly U. Evang. now Unaf. Ch.: One, (104) John[5] W., 1863, m. Ida J. Ferrence. Ch.: One, Charles E., 16 years old.

105.

ELIZABETH[4] GLATFELTER (George[3], &c.), b. Sept. 9, 1831; m. Michael A. Lentz, retired farm. Res. York, Pa. U. Evang. Ch.: Wesley, d. at 2 yrs.; (106) Mary[5] C., 1858, m. Henry C. Sechrist. Ch.: 0.

CHAPTER 3RD. — DANIEL[3].

(107) **DANIEL[3] GLATFELTER** (John[2], Casper[1]). Farmer. Res. Conewago twp. Ch.: (108) Samuel; (109) Daniel; (115) Elija; Jacob, Susan, Elizabeth, all unm.

108.

SAMUEL[4] GLATFELTER (Daniel[3], &c.), moved to Huntingdon co., Pa. Had 2 children, Adam and Samuel, who are married and have children.

109.

DANIEL[4] GLATFELTER (Daniel[3], &c.). Farmer. Conewago twp. Ch.: Rachel and John, both d. unm; (110) Jonas; (111) Daniel B.; (112) Christiana; (113) Emeline; (114) Lucinda.

110.

Jonas[5] Glatfelter (Daniel[4], Daniel[3], &c.), moved to Decatur, Ill., 30 years ago. Had 3 sons: William, Charles, Edward.

111.

Daniel[5] B. Gladfelter (Daniel[4], &c.), res. Conewago twp. Ch. 6: Elmer F., connected with Penna. R. R. Co., is married; Daniel F., unm.; Mary E., d. young; Sarah J. is married; Philip H., m. to un. Middletown, Pa.; inft. daughter, d.

112.

Christianna[5] Glatfelter (Daniel[4], &c.), m. Millard Fetrow, d. Moved to Kansas. Have children.

113.

Emeline[5] Glatfelter (Daniel[4], &c.), is married, res., Wellsville, Pa. Has children.

114.

Lucinda[5] Glatfelter (Daniel[4], &c.), is married. Moved to the West. Have children.

115.

ELIJA[4] GLATFELTER (Daniel[3], John[2], &c.), m. Mary Le Fever. Farm. Ch.: Matilda, unm.; (116) Elias, 1842; (117) John L., (119) Daniel; (120) Eva A.; George, d. at 33; (124) Peter; (125) Mary; Leah, unm.; (126) Samuel; (127) Jane.

116.

Elias[5] Glatfelter (Elija[4], &c.), m. Sarah J. Strominger, d. Res. York, Pa. Pref. Luth. Ch.: 0.

117.

John[5] L. Glatfelter (Elija[4], &c.), 1844, m. Maggie Taylor. Farm at Eberly's Mills, Cumb. co., Pa. Ch.: Herbert, d. unm.; (118) Ada, m. Mr. Haller, Cumb. co., Pa.

119.

Daniel[5] Glatfelter (Elija[4], &c.), 1846; m. Anna Pfaltzgraff. Farm. Res. York, Pa. Ger. Baptist. Ch.: 0.

120.

Eva[5] A. Glatfelter (Elijah[4], &c.), m. Levi Snellbacker, farm. Dover, Pa. Luth. Ch.: (121) Jessie, m. Mr. Benedict; (122) Edward, m. Miss Berkheimer, Doverstown, Pa.; (123) Alice, m. Mr. Pannel, Warrington twp., York co., Pa.

124.

Peter[5] Glatfelter (Elijah[4], &c.), m. Sarah Berkheimer. Res. Dover, Pa. Ch.: 0.

125.

Mary[5] Glatfelter (Elijah[4], &c.), m. Edward Crone, York, Pa. Office cl. & teacher. U. B. Ch.: Bertha and Daisy.

126.

Samuel[5] Glatfelter (Elijah[4], &c.), m. Caroline Gross. Farm. Zion's View, Pa. Luth. Ch.: Minnie, unm. and 4 sons, all dead.

127.

Jane[5] Glatfelter (Elijah[4], &c.), m. Jacob Boaring. Res. near Erney P. O., Pa. U. B. Ch.: One son and 3 daughters.

Chapter 4th. — JACOB[3].

128.

JACOB[3] GLATFELTER (John[2], Casper[1]). Farmer. Resided in Codorus twp. Ch.:

(129) Daniel, 1803;	(200) Mary, 1811–1895 = Bupp;
(143) Jacob;	(207) Sarah = Simmons;
(159) Isaac;	(212) Catharine, 1809–1875;
(166) Jesse;	(219) Lucinda, 1823–1872;
(175) Elizabeth.	

129.

DANIEL[4] GLATFELTER (Jacob[3], John[2], &c.), m. Miss
Ganz. Farm., near Shrewsbury, Pa. Ch.: (130)
Charles; (132) David; Mary, unm.; (132a) Kate, m. Mr.
Hammond, d. Ch.: 0.; Emeline, m. Mr. Wentz, d.
Ch.: 0. (133) Lucinda; (141) Lizzie.

130.

Charles[5] Glatfelter (Daniel[4], Jacob[3], &c.), d. Res. at Glen
. Rock, Pa. Ch.: One daughter; (131), m. to Mr. Morgan.
Res. Philadelphia, Pa.

132.

David[5] Glatfelter (Daniel[4], &c.). Broommaker, Shrewsbury,
Pa. Ch.: One son, John, and a daughter. John, res.
Shrewsbury, Pa., and is a shoemaker.

133.

Lucinda[5] Glatfelter (Daniel[4], &c.), m. Benjamin Keeney,
miller and farm. Tolna, York co., Pa. Ref. Ch.:

Charles H., 1853–1854;	(137) William D., 1861;
(134) John W., 1854;	(138) Catharine R., 1863;
Benjamin F., 1856–1873;	(139) Noah M., 1865;
(135) Daniel E., 1858;	(140) Emma E., 1867;
(136) Anna M., 1860;	Jacob, 1868;

Isaac, 1868–1869.

134.

John[6] W. Keeney (Lucinda[5], Daniel[4], &c.), m. Mary Fife.
Res. Tolna, Pa. Ch.: Grace E., 1886; Edna L., 1888;
Ellis F., 1890; William S., 1891; Laura J., 1895;
Joseph S., 1898.

135.

Daniel[6] E. Keeney (Lucinda[5], &c.), m. Sue Clemenc. Res.
Graydon, Pa. Ch.: Ada M., 1885; Daniel E., 1887;
Benjamin M., 1890; Nora A., 1891; Luther W., 1894;
Celia S., 1896; Emma L. 1898.

136.

Anna[6] M. Keeney (Lucinda[5], &c.), m. John Brose, Stewartstown, Pa. Ch.: Lottie C., 1884; Elsie L., 1889; Melvina F., 1896.

137.

William[6] D. Keeney (Lucinda[5], &c.), m. Emma Reist. Res. Manheim, Pa. Ch.: 0.

138.

Catharine[6] Keeney (Lucinda[5], &c.), m. F. P. Attig. Ch.: Gertrude L., 1891; Florence M., 1893; Marion L., 1895; Carrie E., 1897; Harry C., 1899.

139.

Noah[6] M. Keeney (Lucinda[5], &c.), m. Maude Fife. Ch.: Spurgeon, 1893; Otto M., 1895; Rhoda, 1900.

140.

Emma[6] E. Keeney (Lucinda[5], &c.), m. Geo. Shaub. Res. Tolna, Pa. Ch.: Benjamin M., 1893; Alvin H., 1894; Paul D., 1895.

141.

Lizzie[5] Glatfelter (Daniel[4], Jacob[3], &c.), 1842; m. William Venus. Mngr. furniture f., Shrewsbury, Pa. U. Evang. Ch.: James A., 1870; Chas. H., 1872; Sadie B., 1875; (142) Annie C., 1877; Daniel E., 1880–1897; Ada V., 1883.

142.

Anna[6] C. Venus (Lizzie[5], &c.), m. E. N. Shewell.

143.

JACOB[4] GLATFELTER (Jacob[3], John[2], &c.), m. Sophia Dietrich. Ch.:

(144) Amos D., b. 1835, d. 1898. Catharine, d. at 22.
(149) Rebecca, 1862. George, d. young.
(152) Elizabeth. (157) Jacob, d. 1863, aet. 23.

144.

Amos[5] D. Glatfelter (Jacob[4], Jacob[3], &c.), m. Annie M. Doubler. Res. York, Pa. Carp'r. Luth. Widow, a Meth. Ch.: (145) Ella S., 1861; (147) Charles, 1863; Edward H., 1867–1869; William D., 1869–1869; (148) Annie E., 1870; Calvin F., 1876, unm.

145.

Ella[6] S. Glatfelter (Amos[5] D., &c.), m. William H. Small, York, Pa. Lab. "Protestant," Ch.: Edward, d. inf.; Susan, d.; William A., 1884; (146) Clara, 1882; Harvey C., 1885; Edna, 1900.

146.

Clara[7] Small (Ella[6] S., Amos[5], &c.), m. Nevin Keach, York, Pa. Stone-cutter. Ch.: One, Annie[8] E. (eighth gen.).

147.

Charles[6] Glatfelter (Amos[5] D., Jacob[4], &c.), m. Mary Strickler. Painter. Res. Burlington, N. Jersey. Ch.: 0.

148.

Annie[6] E. Glatfelter (Amos[5], &c.), m. Howard Keach. Ch.: Harold, and one d.

149.

Rebecca[5] Gladfelter (Jacob[4], Jacob[3], &c.), m. Benjamin Hess, York, Pa. Mason. Meth. Ch.: (150) Oliver C., July 11th, 1866; Walter C., 1867; Emma F., 1870; (151) Lillie A., 1873.

150.

Oliver[6] C. Hess (Rebecca[5], Jacob[4], &c.), m. Nellie Brant. Res. York, Pa. Wood-worker. Ch.: One, 1900.

151.

Lillie[6] A. Hess (Rebecca[5], &c.), m. William H. Anderson, York, Pa., salesman. Unaf. Ch.: Mary M., 1894; Paul C., 1896; William A., 1898.

152.

Elizabeth[5] Glatfelter (Jacob[4], &c.), m. George Wehrley, York, Pa., liquor merchant. Ch.: (153) Emma; (154) Sophia; Lizzie; Josephine; George; Charles; (155) Kate; (156) Annie.

153.

Emma[6] Wehrley (Elizabeth[5], Jacob,[4] &c.), m. Mr. Fraley. Ch.: Lizzie and Paul.

154.

Sophia[6] Wehrley (Elizabeth[5], &c.), m. Mr. Gracey, York, Pa. Ch.: James E. and Annie H.

155.

Kate[6] Wehrley (Elizabeth[5], &c.), m. Edward Bentzel, York, Pa. Lawyer. Ch.: Edith, Annie, Edward, Helen, Catherine, Sarah.

156.

Annie[6] Wehrley (Elizabeth[5], &c.), m. Mr. Bratten. Ch.: 0.

157.

Jacob[5] Glatfelter (Jacob[4], Jacob[3], &c.). Ch.: (158) Edward C., 1861; Emma J., 1863, office cl., York, Pa.

158.

Edward[6] Glatfelter (Jacob[5], &c.), m. Jane Fahringer. Baker. York, Pa. U. B. Ch.: Harry G., 1885; Geo. E., 1886, Arthur J., 1889; Paul W., 1898.

159.

ISAAC[4] GLATFELTER (Jacob[3], John[2], &c.), m. Miss Snyder, both d. Res. at Loganville. Lab. Evang. Ch.: One, (160) Anna M.

160.

Anna[5] Mary Glatfelter, (Isaac[4], &c.), m. Noah Goodling, Farm. near Loganville, Pa. She is dead. Ch.:
(161) Ellen M., m. James Dice, Glen Rock. Teacher. Ch.: 3.

(162) Emma, m. Chas. Ramer. Farmer, Loganville, Pa. Ch.: 2.

(163) William, m. Mary Ferree. Carpenter. York, Pa. Ch.: 4.

(164) Edward, m. Catharine Miller. Ch.: 4, one d.

(165) Harvey, m. Annie Hess. Res. Spring Grove. Ch.: 0.

166.

JESSE[4] GLATFELTER (Jacob[3], John[2], &c.). Farm. Winterstown, Pa. Ch.: Isaac[5], 1842–1896, unm.

(167) Jacob[5], m. Miss Waltemeyer. Res. Potosi, Pa. Ch.: 4.

(168) Josiah[5]. Farm. Shrewsbury, m. first, Amanda Erhart, Ch.: Lillie, m. and res. York, Pa.; second, m. Ellen Schweitzer. Ch.: 6; third, m. Miss Trout. Ch.: 1, Ida; Ch. of 2nd marriage, named W. Franklin, Clyde C., Iva L., Ralph R., Myrtle A., and George S.

(169) Sarah[5] J., m. Emanuel Overmiller, auctioneer, York, Pa. Ch.: 1; James, office cl., Spring Grove.

(170) Mary[5], m. Mr. Stouch, saddler, York, Pa.

(171) Levi[5].

171.

Levi[5] Glatfelter (Jesse[4], Jacob[3], &c.). Farm. near Glen Rock, Pa. Luth. Ch.: (172) Alice S., 1864; Emma J., 1865, d.

(173) Edward L., 1866; (174) Chester F., 1869: Annie R., 1871; Mary J., 1873; John H., 1876; Maggie L., 1879; Jennie E., 1881; Cora C., 1886; Katy M., 1888.

172.

Alice[6] Glatfelter (Levi[5], Jesse[4], &c.), m. Noah Mummert. Farm. near Glen Rock, Pa. Ch.: 8.

173.

Edward[6] L. G. (Levi[5], &c.), m. Amanda Rohrback. Ch.: 0.

174.

Chester[6] F. G. (Levi[5], &c.), m. Alice Hildebrand. Ch.: 0.

175.

ELIZABETH[4] GLATFELTER (Jacob[3], John[4], &c.), m. Henry Keesey, farm. Both dead. Evang. Ch.: Matthias, d. young; (176) Mary, 1829; Catharine, 1831, d.; Elizabeth, 1833–1843; (182) Jacob, 1835; (185) Lucinda, b. 1837, d. 1894; Abraham, 1839–1840; (194) Sarah, 1841–1887; Leah, 1844–1857; Charles, 1847–1894.

176.

Mary[5] Keesey (Elizabeth[4], Jacob[2], &c.), m. Adam Stump. Res. Rye, York co., Pa. Luth. Ch.: Miranda, 1853, d. inf.; (177) Adam, 1854; (178) Noah, 1857; Oliver, 1859–1871; (179) Annie E., 1861; (180) Jeanetta, 1864; (181) Samuel, 1868; John H., 1871.

177.

Adam[6] Stump, (Mary[5], Elizabeth[4], &c.), m. Emma O. Yount, of Gettysburg, Pa. Lutheran minister, York, Pa. The Rev. Stump was reared on a farm, taught school, graduated from college 1878, in theology, 1881; served his calling since, partly in Nebraska, but mostly in York co.; is pastor of four churches; besides, a well-known writer of books. Ch.: A. Earl, 1882; Mary O., 1884; Eugene I., 1886; Raymond N., 1888; Theda L., 1891; Florence R., 1894.

178.

Noah[6] Stump (Mary[5], &c.), m. Caroline Wahrenberg. Ch.: Stewart, 1887; Elmer, 1893; Charlotte, 1895; Helen and Ruth, 1897.

179.

Annie[6] E. Stump (Mary[5], &c.), m. Daniel P. Shoemaker. Ch.: Lillie M., 1881; Mary B., 1884; John A., 1887;

William H., 1890–1891; Chas. P., 1892; Lawrence L., 1896.

180.

Jeanetta[6] Stump (Mary[5], &c.), m. Edward Markey. Ch.: Clarence A., 1884; Anna M., 1888; Sarah L. 1891; Geo. A., 1894; Henry C., 1896; Lucy E., 1899.

181.

Samuel[6] B. Stump (Mary[5], &c.), m. Arabella ——. Ch.: Jennie M., 1887; Clarence W., 1890; Ellsworth L., 1895; Mabel G., 1900.

182.

Jacob[5] Keesey (Elizabeth[4], Jacob[3], &c.), m. Elizabeth Stine. Ch.: John H., 1856; Sarah E., 1857; Chas. A., 1860–1871; Edward J., 1867, m.; (183) Jannetta, 1871; (184) Clara I., 1873.

183.

Janetta[6] Keesey (Jacob[5], Elizabeth[4], &c.), m. Ivan Smeich. Ch.: Oscar F. and William N.

184.

Clara I. Keesey (Jacob[5], &c.), m. Chas. Kohler. Ch.: Edward J.

185.

Lucinda[5] Keesey (Elizabeth[4], Jacob[3], &c.), m. Josiah Day. Ch.: (186) Henry C., 1858; (190) Eliza J., 1860; Chas. E., 1863; (189) Susan E., 1865; (191) Geo. A., 1869; (192) Joseph A., 1872; Latimer K., 1874; (193) James K., 1879.

186.

Henry[6] C. Day (Lucinda[5], Elizabeth[4], &c.), m. Sarah L. Stine. Ch.: Howard S., 1877, d. inf.; (187) Martha J., 1879; (188) Leah E., 1880; Clarence D., 1883–1892; Pervilla M., 1885; Alvarous, 1887; Sarah L., 1888; Ida

3

B., 1890; Almeda, 1891; Mabel G., 1892; Mamie E., 1894.

187.

Martha[7] J. Day (Henry[6] C., Lucinda[5], &c.), m. Emory W. Lerew. Ch.: Esther M., b. Oct. 18, 1896; inf. son, Feb. 12, 1898; Roy C., 1900 (8th gen.).

188.

Leah[7] E. Day (Henry[6] C., &c.), m. Augustus F. Reever Ch.: Mocleta, 1897; Cora E., 1898; Kerwin H., 1900 (8th gen.).

189.

Susan[6] E. Day (Lucinda[5], Elizabeth[4], &c.), m. Harry Leber. Ch.: Mamie J., 1890.

190.

Eliza[6] J. Day (Lucinda[5], &c.), m. Aaron Ilyes. Ch.: Carrie M., 1882; Dora E., 1884.

191.

Geo.[6] A. Day (Lucinda[5], &c.), m. Alice Wineka. Ch.: Erwin, 1890; Gertrude, 1892; Masie, 1896.

192.

Joseph[6] A. Day (Lucinda[5], &c.), m. Minnie Heasting. Ch.: Mardella, 1897.

193.

James[6] K. Day (Lucinda[5], &c.), m. Jennie Weitkamp. Ch.: Meda, 1897.

194.

Sarah[5] Keesey (Elizabeth[4], Jacob[3], &c.), m. Edwin Ness. Res. Violet Hill, Pa. Luth. Ch.: Levi, 1862, d. inf.; (195) Chas. W., 1865; (196) Allen E., 1868; (197) Fannie E., 1870; Henry C., 1873; (198) Maurice L., 1875; (199) John L., 1877; Nelson N., 1880; Howard F., 1882.

195.

Chas.[6] W. Ness (Sarah[5], Elizabeth[4], &c.), m. 1st, Lillie
Welty. Ch.: Myrtle; m. 2d, Mary Pipher. Ch.:
Edward.

196.

Allen[6] E. Ness (Sarah[5], &c.), m. Tillie Poff. Ch.: Rufus.

197.

Fannie[6] E. Ness (Sarah[5], &c.), m. Mr. Neff. Ch.: Leon,
John, and Catharine.

198.

Maurice[6] L. (Sarah[5], &c.), m. Sadie Bair. Ch.: Lester.

199.

John[6] L. Ness (Sarah[5], &c.), m. Anna Ferree. Ch.: Helen.

200.

MARY[4] GLATFELTER (Jacob[3], John[2], &c.), m. 1st, Mr.
Bupp. Ch.: (200a) Levi; (201) Sarah, and 2 other children; m. 2d, Michael Crumbling. Ch.: 4. Levi died a
captured prisoner in the Civil War. He was married, had
one son, Eli., now res. State of N. York.
Ch. of 2d marriage are: Mary, d.; (204) Jacob, d.;
(205) W. H.; (206) Amanda.

201.

Sarah[5] Bupp (Mary[4], Jacob[3], &c.), m. Tobias Crumbling,
inventor, machinist, d. 1870. Res. York Co. Ch.:
(202) Edward, 1856; (203) Lincoln E., 1861.

202.

Edward[6] Crumbling (Sarah[5], Mary[4], &c.), m, Arvilla Kise.
Res. Williamsport, Pa. U. Evang. Born in Hellam
twp., 1856, taught school at 16, entered the ministry at 22,

served the Evang. Assoc. until the division, then went
with the U. Evang. and, at present, is in third year.
Presiding Elder, Williamsport District. Ch.: Mary
Edith, 1883; Annie E., 1884; Blanche V., 1886;
Edward N., 1887; Sterling K., 1888; Helen De Etta,
1894–1895.

203.

Lincoln[6] E. Crumbling (Sarah[5], Mary[4], &c.), m. Sarah K.
Krout. Res. Lee's Cross Roads, Cumb. co., Pa. Reared
in York co.; educated in the common and York higher
schools; taught school at 17. After four terms entered
the ministry, U. Evang.; has served the charges at York,
Hanover, &c.; now at Leesburg. Ch.: Carrie A., 1888–
1890; Chas. S., 1891; Mary H., 1893; Edward F.,
1896.

204.

Jacob[5] Crumbling, d. (Mary[4], Jacob[3], &c.), m. Mary Meads.
Was teacher and merchant; widow res. Ill. Ch.: Anna,
Ella, Dora, Oscar.

205.

W. H.[5] Crumbling (Mary[4], &c.). Teacher and painter.
Res. Lancaster city. Ch.: One, Irene.

206.

Amanda[5] Crumbling (Mary[4], &c.), m. Mr. Paet, Hagerstown,
Md. Ch.: Ulysses, Ella, Anna and Franklin, d.

207.

SARAH[4] GLATFELTER (Jacob[3], John[2], &c), m. Mr. Simmons. Ch.: (208) Isaac, d.; m. to un.; left 3 daughters, res. Columbia, Pa.; (209) Aaron[5] I., m. Caroline
Erb. Ch.: One, (210) Aaron[6] I., 1866; (211) Emma[5]
m. Mr. Frymeyer, and res. Brooklyn, N. Y. Ch.: A
number.

210.

Aaron⁶ I. Simmons (Aaron⁵, Sarah⁴, &c.), m. Abbie A. Wolf. Ch.: Caroline A., 1889.

212.

CATHARINE⁴ GLATFELTER (Jacob³, John², &c.), b. Dec. 3, 1809, d. June 17, 1875, buried at Loganville, m. John Werner. Ch.: (213) Jacob, d. 1857, left a son and daughter; John d. unm; Leah d. unm.; (214) Jeremiah.

214.

Jeremiah⁵ Werner (Catharine⁴, Jacob³, &c.), m. Amanda Gallatin. Res. Smith Sta., York co., Pa. Postmaster. U. B. Ch.: (215) George, 1859; John E., 1861–1862; Ellen C., 1862–1872; (216) Albert L., 1864; (217) Jacob A., 1866; William W., 1868–1869; (218) Jeremiah G., 1870; Sarah J., 1871–1872; Carrie, 1872; Mary, 1874; Samuel R., 1876; Edward H., 1878; Harry and Annie, 1880–1881; Emma B., 1882.

215.

Geo⁶. W. Werner (Jeremiah⁵, Catharine⁴, &c.), m. Agnes Lightner. Res. Hanover, Pa. Ch.: A son, Paul.

216.

Albert⁶ L. Werner (Jeremiah⁵, &c.), m. Susie Diether. Res. Willow Grove, Lanc. co., Pa. Butcher. Ref., formerly Evang. Ch.: Lillie M., 1891; Paul G., 1893; Anna S. 1895; Carl G., 1897; Ross W., 1899.

217.

Jacob⁶ Werner (Jeremiah⁵, &c.), m. Estella Ammo. Res. Eufala, Washington. Ch.: Harry J., William and Arthur.

218.

Jeremiah[6] G. Werner (Jeremiah[5], &c.), m. Annie Maurer. Res. Lime Valley, Lanc. co., Pa. Ch.: Harry, Carrie, Jeremiah.

219.

LUCINDA[4] GLATFELTER (Jacob[3], John[2], &c.), m. John Holland, York, Pa. Ch.: (220) Jacob, 1853; (224) a daughter (Mrs. Fields); (225) Catherine E., 1845; (229) Annie, 1844; (229a) a daughter (Mrs. Chas. Wise, York, Pa.); (221) Samuel W., 1852.

220.

Jacob[5] Holland (Lucinda[4], Jacob[3], &c.), m. Mary H. Kohler. Res. York, Pa. Lab. Meth. Ch.: Henry J. 1883; Richard M., 1885; Geo. S., 1887; Mary F., 1893.

221.

Samuel[5] W. Holland (Lucinda[4], &c.), m. Annie K. Eaton. Carpenter, York, Pa. Meth. Ch.: (222) William H., 1875; (223) Bertha L., 1877; John E., 1878; Mary M., 1881; De Etta, 1883; Walter C., 1885; Nora E., 1888; Norman E., 1889; Elmer E., 1892; Catherine P., 1895.

222.

William[6] H. Holland (Samuel[5], Lucinda[4], &c.), m. Eva Showers. Res. York, Pa. Ch.: One, Arthur McKinley, 1898.

223.

Bertha[6] L. Holland (Samuel[5], Lucinda[4], &c.), m. Howard Drayer, chain-maker. Ch.: One, William, 1896.

224.

A daughter (Lucinda, &c.), m. Geo. J. W. Field, Altoona, Pa. R. R. conductor. Meth. Ch.: William C., 1889; Lucinda H., 1891; George J., 1894; Howard J., 1897; Ernest E., 1900.

225.

Catharine[5] Holland (Lucinda[4], &c.), m. Oscar Barnes, lab., Kansas City, Kan. Unaf. Ch.: (226) De Etta, b. 1867, m. Mr. Noble. Ch.: One, Maude; (227) Frank, 1868, married Bertha Hauk. Ch.: None; (228) Frederick, 1871, m. Mamie Hill. Ch.: 0; Judd, 1889.

229.

Annie[5] Holland (Lucinda[4], &c.), m. John W. Culler, machinist, Springfield, Mo. Meth. Ch.: (229a) Charles T., 1867, m. Mary Stoddard; (229b) Annie, 1869, m. L. Stickel. Res. Liberal, Kan. Princ. public schools; George W., 1872; (229c) Laura R., 1874, m. Edgar E. Ennis, traveling salesman (lumber). Ch.: Mary M., 1879; Samuel L., 1881.

CHAPTER 5TH. — SUSAN.

230.

SUSAN[3] GLATFELTER (John[2], Casper[1]), b. July 31, 1794, d. 1868, m. Samuel Forscht, York, Pa. A miller, also sheriff of the county. Ref. Ch.: (231) Henry, 1826–1868; (232) Sarah, 1827, was married. Ch.: 0; Samuel, 1829–1835; (233) Elizabeth, b. 1831; Zachariah, 1833–1861; Susannah, 1835–1838; (239) Israel, 1838; Maria, 1842–1850.

231.

HENRY[4] FORSCHT (Susan[3], John[2], &c.), m. Magdalena[4] Glatfelter (Casper[3], Casper[2], &c.). Ch.: A son, Henry W., d. at 21.

233.

ELIZABETH[4] FORSCHT (Susan[3], John[2], &c.), m. A. J.
Miller, merchant; moved to Savannah, Ga. (1851).
Meth. Ch.: (234) Clayton P., 1854; (235) Preston
H., 1856; (236) Jefferson D., 1865; (237) Robert L.,
1867; (238) Georgie E., 1858. All well educated.

234.

Clayton[5] P. Miller (Elizabeth[4], Susan[3], &c.), m. Ellen Strob-
hart, of Savannah, Ga. Graduate of college, now a
merchant of Savannah. Ch.: Elizabeth F., aet. 23;
Ellen S.; Winifred T.; Sarah B.; Claudia P.

235.

Preston[5] H. Miller (Elizabeth[4], &c.), m. Minnie C. Hudson,
of Nashville, Tenn. Graduate of College. Methodist
minister, now a merchant at Atlanta, Ga. Ch.: A son,
aet. 22. Res. Jacksonville, Fla.

236.

Jefferson[5] D. Miller (Elizabeth[4], &c.), m. Louisa Marmel-
stein. Res. N. Y. City. Salesman. Episc. Ch.:
Georgia E., aet. 12; Jessie W., aet. 16.

237.

Robert[5] L. Miller (Elizabeth[4], &c.), m. Emma Morgan, of
Savannah, Ga. Res. N. Orleans. Salesman. Presby.
Ch.: Henry M., aet. 10; Robert E. L.: Hugh M.;
Herbert M.; inf. dght., 8 mos.

238.

Georgie[5] E. Miller (Elizabeth[4], &c.), m. Lewis W. Thomas,
of Oxford, Ga. Res. now Atlanta, Ga. Lawyer.
Methodist. Ch.: 0.

239.

ISRAEL[4] FORSCHT (Susannah[3], John[2], &c.), m. Elizabeth
Keller. Coach-smith, York, Pa. Ref. Ch.: 0.

CHAPTER 6TH.— EVA.

240.

EVA³ GLATFELTER (John², Casper¹), m. Samuel Raver, farm. Evang. Ch.: (241) Jacob, 1805; (242) Samuel, 1807, d. 1887; (247a) Lydia, m. Adam Snyder, both d.; (see 4) Catharine, m. Peter Glatfelter, both d.; Eva, d. unm.; (247b) Magdalena, d., m., FrederickWalter. Ch.: 0; (248) John, d.; (254) Manasses.

241.

JACOB⁴ RAVER (Eva³, John², &c.). Farmer. Ch.: Wesley, William, Emanuel, and Jacob.

242.

SAMUEL⁴ RAVER (Eva³, &c.), m. Elizabeth Snyder. Farmer. Evang. Ch.: (243) Eli⁵, 1851, m. Susan Neff. Ch.: A son, Erwin C., teacher; (244) Mary⁵, m. Ephraim Krout, d. Ch.: Eli, Frank, Lizzie; (245) Mariah⁵, m. Frank Snyder. Ch.: One; (246) Catharine⁵, m. William Butcher, Dallastown, Pa. Ch.: 2; (247) Sarah⁵, m. Adam Flinchbaugh, Red Lion. Ch.: 1.

248.

JOHN⁴ RAVER, d. (Eva³ John², &c.), m., 1st, Susan Venus, d. Ch.: (249) Frank, m. Miss Bahn. Ch.: 4; Albert, d.; (250) Samuel⁵, m. un. res. Baltimore. Ch.: 3. (251) Frederick⁵, m. un. Ch.: 2; (252) Amanda⁵, m. Joshua Peeling, Batlimore. Ch.: 5; (253) Lizzie, m. Mr. Wilson, Baltimore, Md.; Sons. 2; m. 2nd, Miss Peeling, res. Baltimore. Ch.; 10.

254.

MANASSES⁴ RAVER (Eva³, John², &c.), m. Miss Myers. Blacksmith. Res. Hopewell twp. Ch.: Ellen⁵; (255)

David[5], m. Miss Reichert.   Ch. : 2 ; (256) John[5], m. un.
Ch. : 8 ; (257) Samuel[5], m. Ida Glatfelter (see 29) ; (258)
Jacob[5], m. Miss Snyder.   Ch. : One; Wesley[5], Noah[5],
another son[5], and two daughters[5] all unm.

CHAPTER 7TH. — ROSANNA[3].

259.

ROSANNA[3] GLATFELTER (John[2], Casper[1]), m. Andrew
Ferree, farmer, Spring Garden twp.   Ch. : (260) Israel,
1828; (262) John C., d. ; (264) Henry, d. ; (267) Eliza;
(283) Susannah, m. John Dellinger, d.   Ch.: 0; (270)
Andrew ; (273) Samuel; (279) Lydia.

260.

ISRAEL[4] FERREE (Rosanna[3], John[2], &c.), m. Magdalena
Wallick. Farm near Hellam, Pa. Pref. Ger. Baptist.
Ch. : Henry C., 1856–1867; Amos, 1864–1867; (261)
Milton, 1858; Ida S., 1867–1889.

261.

Milton[5] Ferree (Israel[4], Rosanna[3], &c.), farm., Springetsbury
twp. ; m. Angelina Lehman. Ch. : Mabel A., d. ; Cora
E.; Joseph A.; Harry C. ; Walter I. ; Paul.

262.

JOHN[4] C. FERREE (Rosanna[3], John[2], &c.). Ch.: (262a)
William H.; (262e) Catharine; (263) John L., 1855 ;
(263a) Samuel; (263c) Caleb, m. Elvie Webb, res.
Middleburg, Ohio; (263d) Andrew; (263e) Elizabeth A.

262a.

William[5] H. Ferree, Sen. (John[4] C.,&c.), m. Martha M. Boss-
ler. Res. Rye, Pa. Ch.: (262b) William H., Jun., m.

Callie Mitzel; (262c) Annie M., m. John W. Berger, Spry, Pa.; Charles E.; (262d) John H., m. Kate Eberly; Martha J.; Samuel G.; Sarah E.; Naomi M.

262e.

Catharine[5] Ferree (John C[4]., &c.), m. Adam Flinchbaugh, Dallastown, Pa. Ch.: Elmer; (262f) Maggie, m. Jacob Bates, Dallastown, Pa.; (262g) Susan, m. Frank Winters, same place; (262h) Virgie, m. Wesley Schmuck, Red Lion, Pa.; John A.; Winnie; Paul.

263.

John L.[5] Ferree (John C.,[4] &c.), m. Mary Bupp. Farm. Loganville, Pa. Evang. Ch.: Lillie M. 1898.

263a.

Samuel[5] Ferree (John[4] C., &c.), m. Ellen Reever. Res. Jacobus, Pa. Ch.: (263b) Annie, m. John Ness, York, Pa.; Maggie, Ida, Eli, John, Samuel, Sadie, Daniel, Claudie, Spurgeon.

263d.

Andrew[5] Ferree (John[4] C., &c.), m. Jestina Winters. Res. Middleburg, Ohio. Ch.: Mary, Baltimore, Md.; John, Bonnair, Pa.; Annie, Jefferson, Pa.; Victor, Loganville, Pa.

263e.

Elizabeth[5] A. Ferree (John[4] C., &c.), m. Emanuel H. Ness, Rye, Pa. Ch.: Charles W.; Franklin F.; (263f) Anna M., m. Jacob E. Stump, Red Lion, Pa.; (263g) Robert J.F., m. Laura Brenneman, Glatfelter Sta., Pa.; Samuel; Emma; Emanuel F.; (263h) Sarah E., m. Oliver D. Frey, Red Lion Pa.; Edward E.; William H.; John A.; Andrew E.; Harry W.

264.

HENRY[4] FERREE, d. (Rosanna[3], &c.). Ch.: Six; (265) Andrew[5] has 6 children; (276) Sarah[5], m. Wm. Brenneman, ch. 5; Jeremiah, and 3 others.

267.

ELIZA[4] FERREE (Rosanna[3], &c.), m. Daniel Druck, d. Hellam, Pa. Ch. : (268) Ephraim[5]; (269) Calvin[5] has ch.: Mason[6] and Chauncy[6]; Annie[5], Mary[5], Lydia[5], Leander[5].

268.

Ephraim[5] Druck (Eliza[4], Rosanna[3], &c.), m. Amanda Sheffer, res. Hellam twp. Ch.: Agnes, Andrew, Charles, Kerwin.

270.

ANDREW[4] FERREE (Rosanna[3], &c.), had ch. 2; (271) Albert A., 1847; Rosie A., d.

271.

Albert[5] A. Ferree (Andrew[4], Rosanna[3], &c.), m. Mary A. Knaub. Lab., res. York, Pa. Un. Luth. Ch.: Harry E., 1870; (272) Clara S., 1873; Albert A., 1876; Emma J., 1879; Mary E., d. inf.; Daisie H., 1882; Anna K., 1886; Charles M., 1887; John H., 1890.

272.

Clara[6] S. Ferree (Albert[5], Andrew[4], &c.), m. J. C. Dysinger brakeman R. R. Ch.: 3, one living, John H., 2 yrs. old.

273.

SAMUEL[4] FERREE (Rosanna[3], &c.), m. Catharine Seifert, res. Springetsbury twp. Ch.:
(274) Alice[5], m. Edwin Hively. Ch.: 6.
(275) Annie[5], m. Franklin Bahn. Ch.: 6.
(276) Frank[5], m. Sarah Muckerson. Ch.: 8.

(277) Agnes⁵, m. William Shepp.   Ch.: 1.
(278) Albert⁵, m. Ida Heidelbach.   Ch.: 2.
    Emma⁵ and Dora⁵, unm.

279.

LYDIA⁴ FERREE (Rosanna³, &c.), m. Joseph Dietz, res.
Windsor twp.   Ch.: (280) Clayton⁵, m. Miss Liebhart.
Ch.: One; (281) Ida⁵, m. Mr. Paff.   Ch.: Two; (282)
Moses⁵ is married; Alice⁵, unm.

PART II. — FELIX², AND DESCENDANTS.

283.

FELIX² GLATFELTER, died 1815. He reared his
family on the old Glatfelter farm, near Glatfelter's Sta.,
N. Codorus twp.   A portion of his land possessions was
acquired by two warrants, dated June 8th, 1786; Oct.
4th, 1815.   The executors of his estate were his sons,
Casper and Philip.   The children of Felix were: (284)
Daniel, (385) Philip, (453) John, (515) Frederick,
(527) Barbara, (594) Margaretta, (615) Casper; (629a)
Jacob; (630) Mary; (630b) Elizabeth.
(629a) Jacob³ settled in Tennessee.   Nothing is known of his
    descendants — all connection with his eastern relatives
    appears broken.
(630) Mary³, m. Tobias Hartman.   Ch.: (630a) Rachel⁴,
    m. Geo. Hide; Rebecca, d., unm.; Barbara (no record).
(630a) Rachel⁴, (Elizabeth³, Felix², &c.), m. Geo. Hide,
    farm.   Luth.   Ch.: Leah, 1843–1849; Nancy, 1847–
    1849; John and Susan, d. unm., in Cumberland co., Pa.
(630b) Elizabeth, m. Elusthes Ness.

CHAPTER 8TH.— DANIEL.

284.

DANIEL[3] **GLATFELTER** (Felix[2], Casper[1]), m. Miss Emig. Ch.: (285) Philip G.; (291) Benjamin; (296) Nancy; (313) Susan; (314) George; Dallas, Ch.: 0; (335) Emanuel; (339) Israel; (341) Charles, Jan. 2, 1817, d. 1881; (365) Barbara; (366) Eliza; (384) Rebecca.

285.

PHILIP[4] G. GLATFELTER (Daniel[3], Felix[2], &c.). Ch.: (286) Melinda, 1858; (287) Albert, 1854; (288) Philip; (289) Alice; (290) Sarah A., 1859; Frank, d.; Noah, d.

286.

Melinda[5] Glatfelter (Philip[4] G., Daniel[3], &c.), m. Frank Fishel. Res. Sevenvalley. Luth. Ch.: Harry, 1880, and William, 1882.

287.

Albert[5] Glatfelter (Philip[4] G., &c.), m. Mary Overmiller. Res. Hanover Junction, Pa. Foreman R. R. Luth. Ch.: 0.

288.

Philip[5] Glatfelter (Philip[4] G., &c.), m. Ida J. —— Res. Glatfelter's Sta. Railroader. Luth. Ch.: C. L., 1888; Edward I., 1889; Mary E., 1891; William H., 1893; Sarah E., 1895; Gorman E., 1897; Milliard E., 1900.

289.

Alice[5] Glatfelter (Philip[4] G., &c.), m. A. H. Hake. Sevenvalley. Luth. Ch.: Lillie N., 1887; Lottie M., 1889; Chas. A., 1892.

290.

Sarah[5] A. Glatfelter (Philip[4] G., &c.), m. H. K. Smith. Carp. York, Pa. Ch.: Harry E., 1883; Goldie L., 1888–1888; Raymond W., 1891; Lester A., 1894.

291.

BENJAMIN[4] GLADFELTER (Daniel[3], Felix[2], &c.), m. un. Ch.: (292) Harry I., 1850; (293) Cornelius, 1838–1886; (295) Nathan, 1843; (294) Lucy A., 1855; (296) Amanda, m. Saml. Gayman, Sunbury, Pa.; have four children.

292.

Harry[5] I. Gladfelter (Benjamin[4], Daniel[3], &c.), m. Mary E. Wheeler, of Baltimore. Res. Hanover Junction, Pa. Cig. mnf. Luth. Ch.: 0.

293.

Cornelius[5] Gladfelter (Benjamin[4], &c.), m. Christiana Bricker. Luth. Res. of widow, Hanover Junc. Ch.: Edwin F., 1875–1878; John L., 1876–1878; Henry A., 1878–1878; William H., 1879; Charles C., 1881–1883; Ida M., 1883; Minnie B., 1885.

294.

Lucy[5] A. Gladfelter (Benjamin[4], &c.), m. Henry C. Kuntz, cig. mnf. Sevenvalley, Pa. Luth. Ch.: Harry C., 1874–1876.

295.

Nathan[5] Gladfelter (Benjamin[5], &c.), m. Susan Neff. Res. Sevenvalley. Cig. mnf. Luth. Ch.: Wilford S., 1880; Colstin B., 1882; Neuvia I., 1884; Ives M., 1886; Auburn H., 1888; Linden, 1890.

296.

NANCY[4] GLATFELTER (Daniel[3], Felix[2], &c.), m. Michael Koop, railroader. Luth. Ch.: (297) Lucy, 1835; (301)

Amanda, 1837; (302) Mary A., 1840; (308) Julian, 1842; (309) George, 1844; (310) William, 1846, m. Susan Billit. Ch.: 0; (311) Henry, 1848; Jacob, 1850–1854; (312) Franklin, 1852.

297.

Lucy[5] Koop (Nancy[4], &c.), m. Solomon Falkenstine, farm.; York, Pa. Ch.: Mary[6] A., 1859–1862; (298) Susan[6], 1861, m. Peter Rorbaugh. Ch.: Solomon and Daniel; Henry[6], 1866–1867; (299) Lewis[6] F., 1868, m. Leah Folcomer; (300) Charles[6] C., m. Minnie Henry. Ch.: Raymond and Edward S.

301.

Amanda[5] Koop (Nancy[4], &c.), m. Jacob Danner, Astoria, Ill. Ch.: John, Edward, Daniel, Lovina, Franklin.

302.

Mary[5] A. Koop (Nancy[4], &c.), m. William Hildebrand, shoe m.; Res. Spry, Pa. Luth. Ch.: (303) Margaret[6] S., 1861; John[6], 1863–1868; (304) Isabella[6], 1864; Arabella[6], 1864, m. S. B. Stump (see Keesey fam.); (305) Floretta[6], 1866, m. William Butcher. Ch.: 0; Amanda[6], 1871–1886; (306) Uriah[6], 1868, m. Emmie Smith. Ch.: Mary A., 1893; (307) Wesley[6], 1869, m. to un. Ch.: Edward, 1893; Henry[6], 1873; An[6], inf.; James[6], 1875.

303.

Margaret[6] S. Hildebrand (Mary[5] A. K., Nancy[4], &c.), m. Reuben Stünke. Ch.: Hattie, Reuben, Wesley, Sadie, William, Mary A., and inft. Born 1884 to 1901.

304.

Isabella[6] Hildebrand (Mary[5] A. K., Nancy[4], &c.), m. Jesse Stump, c. m. Luth. Ch.: Mary A., Estara, Henry, Viola.

308.

Julian[5] Koop (Nancy[4], &c.), m. Henry Stambaugh. Res. Spring Forge. Ch.: Nathan, Lucy, William, (d.) Charles, George, Anna, (d.) Ellen. Born, 1865–1885.

309.

George[5] Koop (Nancy[4], &c.), m. Caroline Smith. Ch.: Amanda, William, Lucy, Lillie, Sarah, Albert, Mary.

311.

Henry[5] Koop (Nancy[4], &c.), m. Emeline Gentzler. Res. York, Pa. Ch.: Bert, Cecilia, Jennie, Jacob, Grace. Born 1875–1895.

312.

Franklin[5] Koop (Nancy[4], &c.), m. Lucy Shenberger. Res. Pleasureville, Pa. Ch.: Murray, Carrie, Norman, Harry, Solomon, Emma, Edith.

313.

SUSAN[4] GLATFELTER (Daniel[3], Felix, &c.), m. Mr. Grone. Left two children. Res. unknown.

314.

GEORGE[4] GLATFELTER (Daniel[3], Felix[2], &c.), b. Dec. 26, 1819, d. April 7, 1899. Ch.: (315) Nathaniel, 1848; (316) Wesley, 1849–1893; Nelson, d. at 5 yrs.; (302) Anna M., 1851; (303) Martin, 1853; (322) Queenie A., 1854; Clara, unm., 1855; (307) Theophilus, 1856; (308) Margaret C., 1858; (309) George H., 1860; (311) Jacob, 1861; (312) Christina, 1862; (313) Sarah, 1864; Eliza, 1865, unm.; (314) William F., 1867; (315) Emmeline, 1868; (316) Edward, 1869.

315.

Nathaniel[5] Gladfelter (George[4], Daniel[3], &c.), m. Leah Good. Res. Yantisville, Ill. Farm. Ref. Ch.: Minnie F.,

1874; (315a) William[6] A., 1876, m. Mamie Yost; John
C., 1878; Mary E., 1884; Katy E., 1892.

316.

Wesley[5] Gladfelter (George[4], Daniel[3], &c.), m. Melinda C.
Rohrbaugh. Teacher, Recorder of Deeds. Un. Luth.
Ch.: Warren A., 1874; (317) Laura I., 1877; (318)
Jennie L., 1878; (319) Lizzie A., 1881; Nettie W.,
1883; Clara E., 1885; Edith H., 1888.

317.

Laura[6] I. Gladfelter (Wesley[5], George[4], &c.), m. John Craul.
Res. Dorsey, Md. Ch.: Paul E., aet. 3 yrs.; Ralph K.,
2 yrs.; Catharine E., 1900.

318.

Jennie[6] L. Gladfelter (Wesley, &c.), m. Benton Truitt. Res.
York, Pa. Ch.: 0.

319.

Lizzie[6] A. Gladfelter (Wesley, &c.), m. Wm. Shrive, York,
Pa. Ch.: William M.

320.

Anna[5] M. Gladfelter (George[4], Daniel[3], &c.), m. William
Hosler. Ch.: Mary M., Dora A., Harry, Jansen E.

321.

Martin[5] Gladfelter (George[4], &c.), m. Josephine Hetrick.
Res. Glatfelter's Sta. General merchandise. Luth.
Ch.: 0.

322.

Queenie[5] A. Gladfelter (George[4], &c.), m. William Zink, Cig.
mnf. Manheim, Lanc. co. Ch.: (323) John A., m. Sallie
Whitmeyer; (324) Elsie M., m. Harry A. McCanna.

325.

Theophilus[5] Gladfelter (George[4], &c.), m. Catharine Bortner.
Res. Sevenvalley. Cig. Mnf. Luth. Ch.: Victor A.,

1879; Tillie V., 1881 ; Mabel C., 1885; Althea A., 1897; Harry N., d. young; Otto O., 1883–1891.

326.

Margaret[5] C. Gladfelter (George[4], &c.), m. Jesse Ziegler, lab. York, Pa. Luth. Ch.: Emma, 1880; Charles, 1882; William, 1884 ; Sarah, 1886; Minnie, 1888; John, 1893; Lottie, 1895; Monroe, 1897.

327.

George[5] H. Gladfelter, d. (George[4], &c.), m. Un. Ch.: (328) Noah, 1853 ; Almira, d.; Isabella, d.; George, res. with his mother at New Salem.

328.

Noah[5] Gladfelter (George[5], George[4], &c.), m. Elizabeth Shaibley. Handler l. tobacco, Lanc. city, Pa. Unaff. Ch.: Maggie, 1874–1878; Clara, 1876–1876; Jacob S., 1879; John J., 1881 ; George, 1885; Charles, 1888; Frank, 1890.

329.

Jacob[5] Gladfelter (George[4], &c.), m. un. Res. Manheim, Lanc. co., Pa.

330.

Christina[5] Gladfelter (George[4], &c.), m. Mr. Kuntz. Sevenvalley. Ch.: 0.

331.

Sarah[5] Gladfelter (George[4], &c.), m. Harry Beck, Hotel k., York, Pa. Ch: One.

332.

William[5] F. Gladfelter (George[4], &c.), m. Laura A. Thomas Res. Altoona, Pa. Locom. fireman. Luth. Ch.: Leon T., 1900.

333.

Emmeline[5] Gladfelter (George[4], &c.), m. Chas. Myers, Hanover, Pa. Ch.: 0.

334.

Edward[5] Gladfelter (George[4], &c.), m. un. New Freedom, Pa. Teleg. Op.

335.

EMANUEL[4] GLADFELTER, d. (Daniel[3], Felix[2], Casper[1]), m. Elizabeth Brenneman, now living at New Salem, Pa. He was Justice of the Peace. Luth. Ch.: One (336) Priscilla, d., who m. Clinton Spats. Ch.: (337) Ermie Spats, m. to Claude Smith, N. Salem. Ch.:   Florence; (338) Emanuel Spats, m. to Helen McClure. Graduated physician, res. Hampton, Pa. Luth. Ch.: Mary, 1895.

339.

ISRAEL[4] GLADFELTER (Daniel[3], Felix[2], &c.), m. Catharine Zorbough. Res. Canal-Winchester, Ohio. Stonemason. Ref. Of the family, the only living, and is past 70 yrs. Ch.: Franklin P., 1851, unm.; (340) Elizabeth A., 1855, m. to William D. Beeks.

341.

CHARLES[4] GLADFELTER (Daniel[3], Felix[2], &c.), m. Leah Klinedinst. Res. Codorus twp. Farm. Ch.: (342) Caroline, 1841–1900; (345) Lewis K., 1843; (348) Charles K., 1845; (349) Sevilla, 1846; (354) Ephraim, 1846; (356) Peter K., 1848; (360) Leah; (361) George, 1853; (364) Henry S., 1859.

342.

Caroline[5] Gladfelter (Charles[4], Daniel[3], &c.), m. Michael Stermer, farm. Brodbecks, Y. co., Pa. U. B. Ch.: John, Lucy, Ella, Leah, and 5 dead. Two are married. (343) John[6], m. Rosa Hoff. Ch.: 6; (344) Lucy[6], m. Reuben Warner. Ch.: Alice and Lottie.

345.

Lewis[5] K. Gladfelter (Charles[4], &c.), m. Isabella Kerchner. Res. Neiman, Y. co., Pa. Farm. Luth. Ch.: (346)

Emma[6] J., m. Edward J. Myers. Lawyer. York, Pa. (347) Lucy[6], m. to Dr. Levi M. Bailey; established at Bandanna, Y. co., Pa. Ch.: Jennie[7], Harry[7]. Ch. of Emma[6] J. are Lulu B. and Irene V.

348.

Charles[5] K. Gladfelter (Charles[4], Daniel[3], &c.), m. Eliza Bowman. Farm. Hanover Junct., Pa. Luth. Ch.: Mary J., 1867; Emma, 1869; Minnie, 1872; Howard, 1880; Charles, 1876-1877.

349.

Sevilla[5] Gladfelter (Charles[4], &c.), m. Michael C. Wamer, Neiman, Y. co., Pa. Luth. Ch:
(350) Alice[6], 1866, m. Henry Winters. Ch.: Laura, Emma, John, Mabel, Lottie.
(351) Charles[6], 1867, m. Miranda Layden. Ch.: Lillie.
(352) Rufus[6], 1869, m. Cora Rohrbach. Ch.: Leafy and Ralph.
(353) Lillie[6], 1878, m. Thomas Searles. Ch.: Archibald and Esther; Thomas[6], 1871–1871; Ella[6], 1873–1893; Howard[6], 1881, John[6], 1883; Mollie[6], 1886.

354.

Ephraim[5] Gladfelter (Charles[4], &c.), m. Sarah Krebs. Farm, Brodbeck, Y. co., Pa. Luth. Ch.: Rosa[6], 1876; (355) Luther[6], 1878, m. Laura Kessler. Ch.: a son, John; Harris[6], 1880.

356.

Peter[5] K. Gladfelter (Charles[4], &c.), m. Amelia Bupp. Miller. Neiman, Y. co., Pa. Luth. Ch.:
(357) Mary[6], 1873, m. Howard Sheffer. Ch.: Laura, Oscar, Ralph.
(358) Ella[6], 1875, m. Lewis Caslow. Ch.: Maggie.
(359) Emma[6], 1877, m. Bert Hoff. Ch.: Edna; one[6] d. 1879–1881; Adam[6], 1881; William[6], 1885.

360.

Leah[5] Gladfelter (Charles[4], &c.), m. 1st, Frank Sheffer.
Ch.: Lillie, 1875; Charles, 1880; Bertha, 1886; m.
2nd, Jacob Stermer, farm., Hanover Junct. Luth. Ch.:
Clarence, 1884; Rose, 1885; Ida, 1887; Gussie, 1891;
Minnie, 1893; Harry E., 1894.

361.

George[5] Gladfelter (Charles[4], &c.), m. Clara Klinedinst.
Farm. at Neiman, Y. co., Pa. Luth. Ch.: (362)
Charles[6], 1873, m. Routta Bortner. Ch.: Harry; Ralph;
(363) Alverta[6], 1875, m. Hamilton Kessler. Ch.: 0.
Edward[6], 1876; Robert[6] and Hattie, d.; Gertrude[6],
1882; Olivia[6], 1884; George[6], 1886; Ruth[6] and Bruth,
1892.

364.

Henry[5] S. Gladfelter (Charles[4], &c.), m. Amanda Caslow.
Farm at Neiman. Luth. Ch.: (345) Harry[6], 1880, m.
Cora Keesey. Ch.: 0; Paul[6], 1883.

365.

BARBARA[4] GLATFELTER (Daniel[3], Felix[2], &c.), m.
Jacob Gise. Ch.: Susan, Milton and others. Res. Jackson twp., Y. co., Pa.

366.

ELIZA[4] GLATFELTER (Daniel[3], Felix[2]), m. Henry Bahn,
lab. Luth. ·Ch.: (367) Emeline[5], first, Katie[5], second,
m. Henry Sharp, farm. Luth. Ch.: 0; (368) Sarah[5];
(371) Lucy[5] A.

368.

Sarah[5] Bahn (Eliza[4], Daniel[3], &c.), m. Frederick Rauby,
farm. Luth. Ch.: (369) John; (370) Emma, m. Andrew LeCrone. Ch.: Elsie and another un.

369.

John⁶ Rauby (Sarah⁵ B., Eliza⁴, &c.), m. Agnes Hoffman. Ch.: 10, — Cora, Harvey, Clayton, Edna, Paul, John, Dasie and 3, n. un.

371.

Lucy⁵ A. Bahn (Eliza⁴, Daniel³, &c.), m. Martin Stauch, farm. Luth. New Salem. Ch.: (372) Edward⁶ C.; (373) Sarah⁶ A., m. H. Kline. Ch.: John, Emma, (374) John⁶ C., m. Leah Eyster. Ch. : Peter, Roman, John; (375) Alice⁶ M., m. Chas. Mosberger. Ch.: Michael, Phebe, Emmory; (376) William⁶; (377) Michael⁶; (378) Minnie⁶, m. Latimer Rawhouser. Ch.: Florence, Nettie; (379) Katie⁶, m. Wm. Lentz. Ch.: 0; (380) Emma⁶; (381) Charles⁶, m. Susan Altland. Ch.: Lizzie, Violet; (382) Lucy⁶, m. Wm. Harmon. Ch.: One; (383) Martin⁶, m. Elsie Witmer. Ch.: 0; Jennie⁶, M., d.

372.

Edward⁶ C. Stauch (Lucy⁵ A. B., Eliza⁴, &c.), m. 1st, Lizzie Graybill. Ch.: Curtis, Anna, Paul C., b. 1877 to 1884; m. 2nd, Mary Eply. Ch.: Nettie M., Anna, Lizzie, Sallie, Oliver, Herbert, 1885–1898. Farmer. Luth. Res. Saxville, Pa.

376.

William⁶ Stauch (Lucy⁵ A., Eliza⁴, &c.), m. Sarah Doll. Ch.: Clarence, William, Lottie, Elmer.

377.

Michael⁶ Stauch, (Lucy⁵ A., &c.), m. Henrietta Schindler. Ch.: Mabel, Martin, Walter, Beulah, Michael, inf.

380.

Emma⁶ Stauch (Lucy⁵ A., &c.), m. Charles Cunningham. Ch.: Louisa, Earl, Martin, Allen, Katie.

384.

MARGARET⁴ GLATFELTER (Daniel³, Felix², &c.), m.
Henry Stauffer, age 90 yrs., living with son Franklin,
York, Pa. Luth. Ch.: 8, as follows: (384a) Lucinda,
1838; (384d) Sarah, 1840; (384e) Henry K., 1842;
(384h) Isabella, 1844; (384j) B. Franklin, 1846; Leah,
1851, and Mary A., 1852, d. young; (384n) Alexander,
1854.

384a.

Lucinda⁵ Stauffer (Margaret⁴, Daniel³, &c.), m. Cornelius
Jacobs, farm. East Berlin, Pa. Luth. Ch.: (384b)
Harry⁶, 1872, m. Lizzie Sprenkle. Ch.: Florence; Cur-
tie⁶; (384c) Jennie⁶ S., m. Clarence Ruff. Ch.: Russel;
William⁶.

384d.

Sarah⁵ Stauffer (Margaret⁴, &c.), m. Jacob Loucks, bank
janitor. York, Pa. Luth. Ch.: Charles H., Edward,
William.

384e.

Henry⁵ K. Stauffer (Margaret⁴, &c.), m. Hanna E. Thomas.
Farm. Thomasville, Pa. Luth. Ch.: 15; Luther G.,
1870; Charles M., Maggie K., (384f) Harry L., Lizzie
D., Paul H., Elsie M., Howard A., John F., Elmer C.,
Willis E., Anna G., George W., Jacob M., Robert E.
All born 1870 to 1895. Paul H., (384g) lab. Luth., m.
Jane Brillhart. Ch.: 0.

384f.

Henry⁶ L. Stauffer (Henry⁵ K., Margaret⁴, &c.), m. Minnie
Deardorf. Blacksmith· Luth. Ch.: Russel D., 1895;
Lester R., 1897; Lilian M., 1900.

384h.

Isabella⁵ Stauffer (Margaret⁴, &c.), m. Geo. G. Jacobs, miller;
Jacobs' Mill Sta., Pa. Luth. Ch.: John H. (384i), m.
Anna Wisler, Ch.: Roy and Ralph.

384j.

B. Franklin[5] Stauffer (Margaret[4], &c), m. Emeline Roath. Lab. York, Pa. Luth. Ch.: (384k) Charles H., m. Nettie Heterick; (384l) Lottie M., m. Oliver Gross. Ch.: 2; (384m) Henry H., m. Anna Emig. Ch.: 1.

384n.

Alexander[5] Stauffer (Margaret[4], &c.), m. Anna Hoke. Lab. Luth. York, Pa. Ch.: Berdith, Lillie, Hattie, Henry, Jennie, Rosa.

CHAPTER 9TH. — PHILIP.

385.

PHILIP[3] GLATFELTER (Felix, Casper), b. about 1781, d. 1825; m. Anna M. Emig, who died Dec. 29th, 1878, aet. 95 years. Res. Codorus twp. Ch.: All dead, were as follows: —
(386) Leah, m. Dr. Falkenstine. Ch.: 0.
(387) Jonas, m. 1st, Miss Diehl: 2d, Miss Smyser. Ch.: 3 daughters. Mary, d. 1835, aet. 19; Jacob, d. 1835, at 17 yrs.; (388) Charles; (415) Philip; (424) Jesse, d. 1860, aet. 38; (435) Lydia; (445) Catherine; (446) Rebecca; (452) Elizabeth.

388.

CHARLES[4] GLATFELTER (Philip[3], Felix[2], &c.), m. Louisa Fishel. Farm. Near York, Pa. Luth. Ch.: (389) Jacob, 1835; (392) Philip H., 1837; (395) Edward, 1839; (399) Clementine, 1833–1895; (405) Eliza J.; (408) Anna M.; (411) Louisa, 1846; (412) Emma E.

389.

Jacob[5] Glatfelter (Charles[4], Philip[3], &c.), m. 1st, Margaret
Heid; m. 2d, Miss Hamm. Farm. Res. old homestead.
Luth. Ch.: Charles[6] H., 1859; Clara[6] E., unm.; (390)
William[6] J., m. Miss Hoke. Ch.: 3. One of these
named (391) Sarah[7], m. Mr. Emig; issue, one child
(8th gen.).

392.

Philip[5] H. Glatfelter (Charles[4], Philip[3], &c.), m. Amanda E.
Loucks. Res. Spring Forge, Pa. Paper muf.— one of the
most extensive in the country. Luth. Ch.: (393)
Clara E., 1864; (394) William L., 1865; Mollie I.,
1866; Lucy R., 1872.

393.

Clara[6] E. Glatfelter (Philip[5] H., Charles[4], &c.), m. Charles
E. Moul, Hanover, Pa. Ch.: Elizabeth G., 1890;
Esther G., 1896.

394.

William[6] L. Glatfelter (Philip[5] H., Charles[4], &c.), m. Katha-
ryn R. Hollinger. Res. Spring Forge, Pa. Paper
muf. Luth. Ch.: Philip H., 1889.

395.

Edward[5] Glatfelter (Charles[4], Philip[3], &c.), m. Sarah Herman.
Res. Spring Forge. Superintendent p. mill. Luth.
Ch.: (396) Laura[6] C., 1866; m. William Loucks, freight
agt. Grand Isle, Neb. Ch.: 0. (397) Harvey[6] E.,
1869; m. Nancy Fouts. Res. Central City, Neb. Den-
tist. Ch.: 0. (398) Lucy[6] K., 1871; m. McClellan
Kraft, Spring Forge. Ag't Pa. R. R. Ch.: One, Helen
L. Nettie[6] J., 1873–1892; Sadie[6] E. 1875; unm.

399.

Clementina[5] Glatfelter (Charles[4], Philip[3], &c.), m. George
Shunk, carp. Luth. Ch.: Emma L., 1853; (400)

Mary J., 1855; (401) Charles II., 1856; Jacob II., 1858; (402) Flora E., 1860; (403) Iva A., 1863; (404) George E., 1865.

400.

Mary[6] J. Shunk (Clementina[5], Charles[4], &c.), m. Geo H. Cameron. Res. Walker, Md. Ch.: 11, one d. — Harry G., Benjamin F., Daniel W., Mary C., Francis F., Grover C., Robert L., Anna, Eulah, Joseph, Thos. Van B.

401.

Charles[6] H. Shunk (Clementine[5], &c.), m. Fannie F. Heller. Res. Spring Forge, Pa. Machine hand. Ch.: Nettie P., Beatrice P.; Leona C., George E., Charles B., Elizabeth.

402.

Flora[6] E. Shunk (Clementine[5], &c.), m. L. D. Wiest, res. Portland, Oregon. Civil engineer. Ch.: Marion L., Pauline M., Clementina M.

403.

Iva[6] A. Shunk (Clementine[5], &c.), m. Robert F. Ross, d. Teacher and conductor. Widow, at Spring Forge, Pa. Ch.: Ola, d., and J. Vivian, 1884.

404.

George[6] E. Shunk (Clementina[5], &c.), m. Lillie J. Cisler. Res. Spring Forge, Pa. Machine hand. Ch.: Blanche E., Guy A., Sarah H., Margaret P., d.

405.

Eliza[5] J. Glatfelter (Charles[4], Philip[3], &c.), m. John G. Peters, retired farm. and stock-dealer. York, Pa. Luth. Ch.: (406) Charles L., 1872; (407) J. Frank, 1877; Bertha K., 1869.

406.

Charles[6] L. Peters (Eliza[5] J., Charles[4], &c.), m. Hattie S. Doubler. Res., York, Pa. Helper, paper mill. Luth.

Ch.: Annie M., 1894; Paul G., 1896; Daisie M., 1896; Walter R., 1898.

407.

J. Frank[6] Peters (Eliza[5] J., Charles[4], &c.), m. Carrie C. Greiman. Res., Loganville, Pa. General merchandise. Luth. Ch.: Winona R., 1899.

408.

Anna[5] M. Glatfelter (Charles[4], Philip[3], &c.), m. Benjamin Myers, d. Ch.: (409) Annie, m. Jacob Miller, Jackson twp. Ch.: 4; (410) Harry, m. to un. Salesman, York, Pa. Ch.: 2.

411.

Louisa[5] E. Glatfelter (Charles[4], &c.), m. John A. Eyster, paper m. hand. Spring Forge. Luth. Ch.: George F., 1868.

412.

Emma[5] E. Glatfelter (Charles[4], &c.), m. Samuel S. Forrey. York, Pa. Luth. Ch.: (413) Annie K., 1872, m. William R. Gotwalt; Charles H., 1873–1873; (414) Latimer G., 1874–1899, m. Minnie Doll; William Luther, 1876–1876; Harvey E., 1878.

415.

PHILIP[4] GLATFELTER, d. (Philip[3], Felix[2], &c.), m. Catharine Geiselman. Widow, res. at Old Homestead, Sevenvalley. Luth. Ch.: Elenora[5], d.; George[5], d.; (416) Emmeline[5], m. Wm. Martin. Ch.: 8; (417) Jestina[5], 1849; (418) Lillie[5], 1850; (419) Rosie[5], 1858, m. Samuel L. Gross, carp. York, Pa. Ch.: 0. (420) Mahala[5], 1861, m. Geo. E. Holtzapple, M. D., York, Pa. Ch.: Gertrude S.; Edward[5], d.; (421) Sarah[5] A.; William[5], d.; (422) Robert[5], m. Marie Shock. Vet. surg. Phila., Pa. Ch.: Aline M., 1889, and Robert, 1896.

417.

Jestina[5] Glatfelter (Philip[4], &c.), m. Pius W. Wonner, printer, York, Pa.; U. Luth. Ch.: (417a); Wilbert W., 1875, m. to Elsie Hummel. Teleg. Op., Hanover, Pa. Ch.: 0.; Clarence W., 1876; Daisie G., 1877; Edwin R., 1888.

418.

Lillie[5] Gladfelter (Philip[4], &c.), m. Allen Gladfelter, M. D., (d.); widow, res. Sevenvalley. Ch.: Olivia.

421.

Sarah[5] H. Gladfelter (Philip[4], &c.), m. William W. Bott, lab. York, Pa. Luth. Ch.: Elsie M., 1870; William A., 1873; Rosie V., 1881.

423.

JESSE[4] GLATFELTER (Philip[3], Felix[2] &c.), m. Matilda Smith. Farm. Res. York co., Pa. Luth. Ch.: (424) Nathan S., 1846; (426) Philip J., 1852; (410) Louis W., 1854, (414) Jonathan A., 1856; Emmeline, m. David B. Glatfelter (Jacob[3], Henry[2]).

424.

Nathan[5] S. Gladfelter (Jesse[4], Philip[3], &c.), m. Anna M. Metzger, Res. Steubenville, Ohio, paper-maker. Meth. Ch.: (425) Grace M., 1869; m. John McCracken; Jesse M., 1874; Frederick A., 1877; Harry R., 1882.

426.

Philip[5] J. Gladfelter (Jesse[4], &c.), m. Susan Bahn, res. Spring Forge, Y. co. Pa. Paper finisher. Luth. Ch.: (427) Lillie M., 1872; Jesse F., 1875–1880; Bert A., 1878; Daisie M., 1880.

427.

Lillie[6] M. Gladfelter (Philip[5] J., Jesse[4], &c.), m. Valentine Crone, Spring Forge, Pa. Ch.: Edwin V., Winfield S., Joseph P., Stella V., Mary A.

428.

Louis[5] W. Gladfelter (Jesse[4], Philip[3], &c.), m. Melinda Warner. Res. Sevenvalley, Y. co., Pa. Lab. Luth.
Ch.: (429) Jestie[6] A., 1873, m. Fred. M. Bupp, Sevenvalley. Luth. Ch.: One, Fairie M., 1893. (430)
Cora[6] M., 1876, m. Wm. L. Searle, Sevenvalley. Luth.
Ch.: William L., 1894; Eugene, 1897; Guy, 1900;
(431) Ida[6] M., 1879, m. C. W. Klinedinst; Mary[6] A.,
1882; Jessie[6] C., 1884; John[6] R., 1887; Myrtle[6] I.,
1891; L. Walter[6], 1894; Raymond[6], 1896.

432.

Jonathan[5] A. Gladfelter (Jesse[4], Philip[3], &c.), m. Sarah A.
Harbold. Res., York, Pa. Blacksmith. Luth. Ch.:
Charles A., 1881; (433) Warthy N., 1879, m. Michael
Merkle, Res. Jacobus, Pa.; Tillie L., 1884; Elsie V.,
1888; Lillie, 1889; Jesse, 1893; Minnie M., 1875, d.

434.

LYDIA[4] GLATFELTER (Philip[3], Felix[2], &c.), m. Wm. Diehl.
Ch.: (435) John, m. Miss Kohler. Res. Glen Rock.
Ch.: 5; (436) Amanda m. John Hamm, Bair's Sta., Pa.;
Ch.: 5; (437) Melinda, 1834; (441a) Jacob, Res. Seven-
valley, m. Miss Walter. Ch.: 2; (442) Jeremiah; (443)
Martin; (444) William; Nathaniel, unm.

437.

Melinda[5] Diehl (Lydia[4], Philip[3], &c.), m. Jacob Schepp,
farm. Brillhart Sta. Luth. Ch.: Louisa[6] A., 1857–
1861; Mary[6] A., 1858–1859; (438) Alice[6], 1861, m.
David M. Gentzler, salesman, York, Pa. Luth. Ch.:
Thomasa S., 1883–1892; Paul S., 1886; Bertha V.,
1887; David, 1888; Elmer, 1890; William, 1891;
Martha[6] J., 1860–1861; (439) Nelson[6], d. 1863, m.
Carrie Weiser. Ch.: 7; (440) Elizabeth[6], 1865, m.
Clayton Strickhauser, York, Pa. Ch.: 3; William[6],

1866; (441) Lydia⁶, 1872, m. Allen Loader, preacher, Richmond, Ind. Ch.: One. Emmeline⁶, 1876, unm.

442.

Jeremiah⁵ Diehl (Lydia⁴, Philip³, &c.), m. Miss Garver. Resided in Lanc. co., Pa. Soldier, killed in battle, Civil War. Ch.: 3.

443.

Martin⁵ Diehl (Lydia⁴, &c.), m. 1st, Christina Fishel; 2nd, Catharine Matson. Res. York, Pa. Auctioneer. Ch.: 16.

444.

William⁵ Diehl (Lydia⁴, &c.), m. Miss Diehl, a cousin. Res. Nimecola, Summit Co., Ohio. Ch.: 9.

445.

CATHARINE⁴ GLATFELTER (Philip³, Felix², &c.), m. Jonas Folckommer. Left one son and two daughters.

446.

REBECCA⁴ GLATFELTER (Philip³, &c.), m. Michael Gentzler. Left a daughter Lucy, m. to (447) Daniel Widman, farm. Thomasville, Pa. Luth. Ch.: (448) William⁶, 1885, m. Sarah Lau. Ch.: Luther; (449) Edward⁶, m. Ellen Holtzapple. Ch.: Isabella M. and Charles D.; (450) Franklin⁶, (d.), m. Isabella Senft. Ch.: Charles D.; (451) Jane⁶, m. Charles Eyster. Ch.: Henry and George D.; Minnie⁶, 1880, unm.

452.

ELIZABETH⁴ GLATFELTER (Philip³, Felix, &c.), m. John Wagner. Ch.: 5 sons and 2 daughters.

Chapter 10th. — JOHN.

453.

JOHN³ GLATFELTER (Felix, Casper). Res. Codorus
twp. Ch.: 10, as follows: (454) Jacob⁴; (464) Frederick⁴, to Ill., m. Miss Gildauer; (465) (Joseph⁴, to Ill.;
(466) John⁴; (499) Samuel⁴; (478) Daniel⁴ J., Sept. 29,
1820; (509) Barbara⁴, m. H. King; (510) Sarah⁴ G.,
1818–1871; (512) Elizabeth⁴, m. Thomas Erhart; (513)
Mary⁴ m. Jacob Gentzler. Ch.: (514) Emanuel⁵, said
to have Ch. 17.

454.

JACOB⁴ GLATFELTER (John³, Felix, &c.), m. Lydia
Folckommer, who d. 1893, aged 93 yrs. Ch.: (455)
Franklin, 1824; (455a) Sarah, m. Jesse Beaker. Ch.: 0.;
Levi, d.; (460) Lydia.

455.

Franklin⁵ Glatfelter (Jacob⁴, John³, &c.), m. 1st Rebecca
Smith; m. 2nd Frances A. Ernst. Res. New Salem.
Tailoring and farm. Luth. Ch.: 1st wife, are Emeline,
1846, d.; (456) Salina, 1848; Jacob, 1852, d.; (458)
Theodore, 1855, office cl., m. Emma Lehr (d.). Ch.: 0;
Amanda, 1859, d.; (459) Luther, 1850; (459a) Alwin,
1864, m. Miss Stanley. Ch.: Carl S. Children of 2nd
w., Martha, 1884, d., and Mabel B., 1889.

456.

Salina⁶ Glatfelter (Franklin⁵, Jacob⁴, &c.), m. Mr. Kauffman,
res. Spring Forge, Pa. Luth. Ch.: Twins, 1869, d.;
(457) Harry U., 1870; Minnie, 1872–1874; Paul S.,
1875; Luther F., 1877–1896; Rebecca S., 1879; Lucy
K., 1882; Jennie E., 1885–1891; Winnie, 1888.

457.

Harvey[7] U. Kauffman (Salina[6], Franklin[5], &c.), m. to un. Ch.: Walter[8] C., March 15th, 1894, and Abraham[8] F., Sept. 28th, 1899. (8th gen.)

458.

Theodore[6] Glatfelter (Franklin[5], Jacob[4], &c.), m. Emma Lehr, d. recently. Office cl. Luth. Ch.: 0.

459.

Luther[6] Glatfelter (Franklin[5], &c.), m. Eliza J. Hake. Genl. merchse. York, Pa. Luth. Ch.: Chas. W., 1884; Gertrude I., 1887; Bessie E., 1889; Fred. F., 1892; Sallie R., 1896.

460.

Lydia[5] Glatfelter (Jacob[4], John[3], &c.), m. John S. Kline. Ch.: 4: (461) Julia[6], m. Mr. Feistel, N. Salem. Ch.: 0; (462) Frank[6], m. to un. York, Pa. Ch.: A number; (463) Sarah[6], m. Geo. Gibbons, New Salem, Pa. Ch.: J. Harry[7]; Henrietta[6], d.

466.

JOHN[4] GLATFELTER (John[3], Felix[2], &c.), m. Regina Folckommer. · Ch.: (467) Annie, m. John Messersmith, York, Pa. Ch.: 4; (468) Agnes, m. Peter Stouch (d.), York, Pa. Ch.: 3. (469) Eliza M. Geo. Dehoff, Columbia, Pa. Ch.: 3; (470) Lydia, m. Chas. Ness, York, Pa. Ch.: 2; (471) Polly, m. Henry Seneft, Brillhart's Sta., Pa.; Emanuel d. unm.; (472) Kate (d.), m. John Truitt (d.), York, Pa. Ch. 2; Belle[5], unm; Jacob[5], d. young; (473) Julia[5] A., m. Taylor S. Gable, York, Pa. Genl. Merchse. Luth. Ch.: Harry, 1871, William, 1872, Morris, 1873; (474) John[5] H (d.).

474.

John[5] H. Glatfelter (John[4], John[3], Felix[2], &c.), m. Christina Altland. Ch.: (475) Robert, m. Mary E. Jacobs who has

Ch.: 2: Helen L., 1898, and William E., 1899; (476) Harry, carriage tr., m. Annie Lentz. Ch.: 1; (477) Lila, m. Wm. Roy, Baggage-master, Columbia, Pa. Ch. Ethel, Ida, Ralph.

478.

DANIEL[4] J. GLATFELTER (John[3], Felix[2], &c.), m. Sarah Emig (d.). Farm. near Brillhart's Sta., Pa. Luth. Ch.: 16, as follows: (479) 1, William G., 1840; 2, Mary, 1842, d. young; 3, Susannah, 1843; 4, John, 1844, was m. Ch.: 0; (484) 5, Jacob, 1846; (488) 6, Dallas, 1847–1887; (491) 7, Franklin, 1849; m. to Miss Gentzler; has 7 children; 8, Sarah J., unm.; (492) 9, Alonzo, 1852, Ch.: 9; (493) 10, George, 1854; (495) 11, Melvina, 1855; 12, Daniel, 1859–1861; 13, Harry, 1858 d. young; (496) 14, Margaret, 1861; (497) 15, Lydia, 1863; (498) 16, Ellen R., 1865, m. F. Klinedinst. Ch.: 6.

479.

William[5] G. Glatfelter (Daniel[4] J., John[3], &c.), m. Sarah A. Klinedinst. R. R. lab. Sevenvalley. Luth. Ch. 12: (480) Charles, 1867, m. Annie Keim. Res. Sevenvalley. Ch.: Mary and Sarah; William, 1870; (481) Albertus, 1872; (482) Robert D., 1874, c. m. Hanover Junction, m. Abbie Hewett. Ch.: Bessie M , 1894; Mariah, 1897–1899; (483) George; Joseph, d. 3 yrs. old; Howard, 1879; John, 1891; Louis, d. at 15; Claudia, 1885; Minnie, 1887; Gertie V., 1891.

481.

Albertus[6] Glatfelter (William[5] G., Daniel[4] J., &c.), m. Annie L. Ernst. Res. Sevenvalley. c. m. Luth. Ch.: Ralph A., 1890; Glen R., 1894; Earl E., 1896; Lelia B., 1898; Louis W., 1899.

483.

George Glatfelter (William G., &c.), m. Lestie Warner. Res. Sevenvalley, Pa. Ch.: Evan, Ida, Ada.

484.

Jacob[5] Glatfelter (Daniel[4] J., &c.), m. to un. Ch.: 7:
Harry, unm.; Kerwin, unm.; (485) Edward, m. Annie
Moyer. Ch.: 3 daughters; (486) Nerva, m., Mr. Shetter.
Ch.: Myrtle, Roy, Clare, Raymond; (487) Alice, m. Mr.
Tupper. Ch.: Myrla; Bertha J., unm., York, Pa.;
Levi, unm.

488.

Dallas[5] Glatfelter (d.) (Daniel[4] J., &c.), m. Louisa Emig,
now res. at New Salem, Pa. Ch.: (489) Sarah A.,
1869, m. Mr. Ness; (490) Evan, 1871; (491) Sophia,
1873, m. Mr. Zortman; John, 1875; James, 1877; (492)
Maggie K., 1880, m. Mr. Gentzler; Charles, 1882;
Tillie, 1885.

490.

Evan[6] Glatfelter (Dallas[5], Daniel[4] J., &c.), m. Claudie
Ness. Coachman for P. A. and S. Small, York, Pa.
Ch.: 0.

492.

Alonzo[5] Glatfelter (Daniel[4] J., &c.), m. Miss Fried. Res.
Stonybrook, Pa. Ch.: 9.

493.

George[5] Glatfelter (Daniel[4] J., &c.), went West, died there,
had two sons, James and (494) Harvey W., res. Manchester, Pa. Ch.: Katy.

495.

Melvina[5] Glatfelter (Daniel[4] J., &c.), m. Geo. Fishel, who is
in hospital at Harrisburg. Wife res. with her father.
Ch.: Elmer C., Robert, John, and Virgie.

496.

Margaret[5] Glatfelter (Daniel[4] J., &c.), m. Geo. A. Butcher,
farm., Brillhart Sta., Pa. Ref. Ch.: Bertha J., 1880;

Daisie M., 1882; Charles, 1884; Sadie, 1886; Minnie,
1888; Carrie, 1891; Rosie, 1894; Sarah, 1896; George,
1898; Violetta, 1900.

497.

Lydia[5] Glatfelter (Daniel[4] J., &c.), m. John A. Ziegler,
carp. N. York, Pa. Luth. Ch.: 11: Robert P., Annie
K., Daniel E., Sadie M., Lucy R., Elenora, Ada A.,
Lydia V., John H., d. 1887; Gertrude E., d.; Harry F.,
d. All b. from 1882 to 1898.

499.

SAMUEL[4] GLATFELTER (John[3], Felix[2], &c.), m. Elizabeth Arman. Res. Lanc. co., Pa. Ch.: 11, as follows:
(500) Horace A., 1833; (501) Zacharias, (d.), res.
Ill.; (502) Martin, m. to un., res. Mt. Union, Huntingdon
co., Pa.; (504) Samuel; Maggie, d.; (505) Isabel,
m. John Smyser, Marietta, Pa.; Mariah, unm., res. Harrisburg, Pa.; (506) Matilda, m. M. Liphart (d.), Lanc.
city, Pa.; (507) Elizabeth, m. John I. Jacobs, res.
Withawn, Ark.; (508) Malinda, m. Edward Bohm, res.
Phila., Pa.; Catharine, unm., resides with Edw. Bohm.

500.

Horace[5] A. Glatfelter (Samuel[4], John[3], &c.), m. 1st to Elizabeth Hollinger, who d. 1886; m. 2nd to Barbara Weaver,
also dead. Farmer, at Maytown, Lanc. co., Pa. Unaf.
Ch.: John W., 1861–1861; Samuel, 1863–1864; William, 1865–1873; (500a) Horace, 1867, m. Emma Baus-
tick. Ch.: One, Erwin, 2 yrs. old; Ella, 1890.

504.

Samuel[5] Glatfelter (Samuel[4], John[3], &c.), Prop. Franklin
Hotel, Columbia, Pa. Ch.: (504a) George S., 1868,
m. to un. Ch.: James W., 1894; Genevieve, 1897;
William A., 1870., unm.; (504b) Harry B., 1872, m. to
un. Ch.: 2.

510.

SARAH[4] G. GLATFELTER (John[3], Felix, &c.), m. Charles Neff, who died 1900 at 89 yrs., res. Dallastown, Pa. Ch.: 11. All but one, viz., Sarah G., 1840, died young. (511) She m. Dr. Samuel S. Lawson, Dallastown. Ref. Ch.: 2: an inft. (d.), and Thomas A., 1879, attending college at Annville, Pa.

CHAPTER 11TH. — FREDERICK.

515.

FREDERICK[3] GLATFELTER, 1795–1856 (Felix[2], Casper[1]), m. Dorothy Swarts. Cooper and farmer, W. Manches twp. Ref. Ch.: (516) Granville, March 7th, 1836; (518) Dietrich, 1826–1900; (519) Anna M., 1841.

516.

GRANVILLE[4] GLATFELTER (Frederick[3], &c.), m. Catharine Hamm. Farm. near Brillhart's Sta., Pa. Ref. Ch.: (517) Emma J., 1866; Oliver E., 1868, grad. of Pa. State Normal School; Milton H., 1870; Martha, m., 1872–1876; Clayton H., 1875; Herbert R., 1877; Alice O., 1879; Oscar J., 1882; Pervilla C., 1884.

517.

Emma[5] J. Glatfelter (Granville[4], Frederick[3], &c.), m. Pius R. Hess, carp., York, Pa. Ref. Ch.: Ada, 1894, Lester, 1897, and Laura C.

518.

DIETRICH[4] GLATFELTER (Frederick[3], &c.), m. Elizabeth Seitz. Farm., York twp. Ref. Widow, res. York, Pa. Ch.: Elenora, 1853–1876.

519.

ANNA[4] M. GLATFELTER (Frederick[3], &c.), m. Solomon
Fahs, farm., York, Pa. Luth. Ch.: 11, as follows:
(520) Lucy[5] E., 1860, m. Mr. Rupert, farm., Dover
twp. Ch.: Rosa, 1880; William, 1885; (521) Franklin[5] P., 1861, m. Amanda Wolfort, Jackson twp.
Ch.: Harry, 1885; Kerwin, 1887; (522) Catharine[5],
1862, m. John May, Dover twp. Ch.: Alice;
(523) Charles[5] E., 1863, m. Martha Beck. Tinner,
Jacobus, Pa. Luth. Ch.: 0. (524) Henry[5], 1866;
(525) Emma[5], 1870, m. Edw. Bupp, York twp.; farm.
Luth. Ch.: Mabel, 1894. (526) Allen[5] L., 1872, m.
Jennie Bupp. Tinner, Myersville, Pa. Luth. Ch.: 0;
Mary[5] A., 1874, and Rosa[5] J., 1876, unm.; Amand[5] J.,
1863–1863; Clayton[5] H., 1877–1878.

524.

Henry[5] Fahs (Anna[4] M., Frederick[3], &c.), m. Anna Markey.
Res. York twp. Ch.: Sadie, 1889; Clayton, 1892;
David, 1895; Amanda, 1899.

Chapter 12th.— BARBARA.

527.

BARBARA[3] GLATFELTER (Felix[2], Casper[1]), m. Jacob
Hovis, farm. Luth. Ch.: (528) Daniel, 1809; (529)
Catharine, 1812; (530) Rachel, 1814; (539) Isaac,
1816; (552) Jacob, 1819; (568) Elizabeth, 1821–1893;
(581) Jesse, 1823; Adam, d. young; (587) Franklin,
1827.

528.

DANIEL[4] HOVIS (Barbara[3], Felix, &c.), m. Frena Glatfelter, daughter of Philip, of Henry. Farm. Luth.

Moved to Juniatta co., Pa. Had 12 ch.: Isaac, Daniel,
Louisa, Franklin, Jacob, Fanny, Lizzie, Barbara, inf.,
and 3 names un. All live in Juniatta and Snyder co's.
except a son, went West.

529.

CATHARINE[4] HOVIS (Barbara[3], &c.), m. Conrad Markle,
farm. and surveyor. Luth. Parents dead. Ch.:
Henry, Isaac, Franklin, res. in Clearfield co., Pa. These
have children and grandchildren; also 3 daughters:
Leah, Lucy, d. young, Catharine, m. to un. Res. Ill.

530.

RACHEL[4] HOVIS (Barbara[3], &c.), m. Samuel Hess, farm.
Ref. Ch.: (531) Isaac, 1837–1887; (532) William,
1839; (537) Mary A., 1840–1892; Eliza, 1842; Sarah
E., 1844; Michael, 1846–1900; Jacob P., 1848; (538)
Clara J., 1856.

531.

Isaac[5] Hess (Rachel[4] Hovis, Barbara[3], &c.), m. Mary J. —.
Res. Chicago. Ch.: Sadie, 1870; Emma, 1872; Elizabeth, 1878.

532.

William[5] Hess (Rachel[4], &c.), m. Miss Conaway. Farm.
York co., Pa., U. B. Ch.: 12; (533) Mary J., 1861;
Benjamin F., 1863–1863; Agnes E., 1864; (534) Will-
iam H., 1866; Sarah E., 1868–1875; Aaron C., 1870;
(535) Samuel F., 1873; Daniel C., 1875–1875; (536)
Clara J., m. Elmer Boeckel, farm., Spry, Pa., U. B.
Ch.: An inft.; Edward C., 1879–1879; Milton J., 1881;
Elmer M., 1885–1886.

533.

Mary[6] J. Hess (William[5], Rachel[4], &c.), m. Henry Smith,
Spry, Y. co., Pa., U. B. Ch.: Leon, 1886; Millie A.,
1896.

534.

William[6] H. Hess (William[5], Rachel[4], &c.), m. to un. Farm.
U. B. Spry, Pa. Ch.: Frederick W., 1889; Lillie M.,
1890 ; Aaron F., 1893; Sarah A., 1896; Mabel E., 1899.

535.

Samuel[6] F. Hess (William[5], &c.), m. Farm. Spry, Pa.
U. B. Ch.: David C., 1896; Aaron C., 1898; Geo.
H., 1900.

537.

Mary[5] A. Hess (Rachel[4], Barbara[3], &c.), m. Michael Lighty,
lab., Chicago, Ill. Luth. Ch.: John, Minerva, Elmer,
Samuel, Edward, born 1865 to 1879.

538.

Clara[5] J. Hess (Rachel[4], &c.), m. Edward Ness, carp. York,
Pa. U. B. Ch.: Sadie E., 1889; James, 1892; Lillie,
1894.

539.

ISAAC[4] HOVIS (Barbara[3], Felix[2], &c.), m. Eliza Peters.
Farm. Luth. Ch.: Jacob, 1846 (d.); (540) Susan,
1848; (545) Mary C., 1850; (550) Eliza, 1853 (d.);
Barbara E., 1855, d.; Clara I., 1859, d.; Isaac P., 1862,
d.; William H., 1865.

540.

Susan[5] Hovis (Isaac[4], Barbara[3], &c.), m. Jacob Hoke, farm.
New Salem, Pa. Luth. Ch.: William[6], 1868–1868;
(541) Lucy[6] E., 1870; m. Mr. Holtzapple, lab. Ch.:
Naomi and Lucy E.; John[6], 1875–1880; (542) Mary[6]
E., 1872, m. John Ziegler, farm., Sevenvalley. Luth.
Ch.: 0; (543) Isaac[6] H., 1877, m. Miss Decker.
Farm. N. Salem. Luth. Ch.: One, Jeanette L., 1900;
(544) Anna[6] M., 1879, m. William Swarts, merch. N.
Salem. Ch.: One, infant.; Sadie[6] S., 1881; Michael[6],
1883; Masie[6] K., 1886.

545.

Mary[5] C. Hovis (Isaac[4], &c.), m. John Ilyes, farm., Brillhart, Pa. Luth. Ch.: 12; (546) Ida[6] J., 1868; Ellen[6] V., 1870–1870; Annie[6] E., 1872–1872; (547) Albert[6] G., 1873, m. Ida Kohler. Farm., Brillhart Sta. Luth. Ch.: Percy[6] A., 1898; (548) Clannie[6] E., 1875, m. Leander Minnich, farm. Brillhart Sta. Luth. Ch.: Clarence R., 1899; (549) John[6] F., 1877, m. Mary Boyer. Farm. Brillhart Sta. Luth. Ch.: Wilson B., 1899–1900, and Jestina E., 1900; William[6] H., 1879; Henry[6] S., 1881; Edward[6] I., 1883; Belle[6] N., 1886; Lottie[6] V., 1890; Geary[6] A., 1895.

546.

Ida[6] J. Ilyes (Mary[5] C., Isaac[4], &c.), m. Cornelius Lentz, farm. Glatfelter's Sta. Luth. Ch.; Inf't (d.); Mabel, 1889; Erwin, 1893; Vernia, 1897; Walter, 1899.

550.

Eliza[5] A. Hovis (Isaac[4], Barbara[3], &c.), m. Mr. Ness, lab. Luth. Ch.: Kerwin, Luther, Alveta, Isabel (d.). Ages 6 to 15 years.

551.

William[5] H. Hovis (Isaac[4], &c.), m. Miss Williams. Farm. Luth. Ch.: Annetta, d.; Anna M., Ellen, Etta K., Elizabeth, Isaac W. (d.). Ages 1 to 10 years.

552.

JACOB[4] HOVIS (Barbara[3], Felix), m. Mariah Peters. Farm. Luth. Ch.: 12: (553) Sarah[5], 1843; James, 1844–1899; (557) Barbara[5] E., 1846; (559) Elizabeth[5] C., 1849; (563) Oliver[5] F., 1851, m. Barbara A. Workinger. Farm. Luth. Ch.: Maggie M., and Elmer P.; (564) Annie[5] M., 1853, m. to un. Ch.: Nellie, 1880, and Martin, 1882; (565) Alevia[5] J., 1855, m. Milton Sakemiller, salesman, York, Pa. Luth. Ch.: Harry, 1879, and

Jennie, 1882; Jacob[5], 1858, d.; Edward[5] D., 1860, unm.;
Charles[5], 1861, d.; (566) Emma[5] L., 1863, m. Harry;
Stabley, c. m., Spry, Pa. Luth. Ch.: Blanche, 1892,
and Paul, 1894; (567) Alice[6], 1867, m. Wm. Sprenkle,
c. packer. Loganville. Luth. Ch.: George L., 1886,
and William J., 1894.

553.

Sarah[5] Hovis (Jacob[4], Barbara[3], &c.), m. Isaac Leader.
Farm. Spry, Pa. Luth. Ch.: (554) Elenora[6], 1866,
m. Wm. Kornbauer. Farm. Luth. Ch.: Edward F.;
(555) Harry[6] J., 1876, m. Ida Hoffman. Farm. Spry,
Pa. Luth. Ch.: Charles; (556) Lizzie[6] M., 1883, m.
Noah Inerst. Farm. Luth. Ch.: one, Grace; Maggie[6],
1869–1875; Frederick[6] A.

557.

Barbara[5] A. Hovis (Jacob[4], &c.), m. Adam Keesey, teleg.
op., York, Pa. Luth. Ch.: (558) Clarence[6] A., m.
Hattie Lafane. Clerk. York, Pa. Luth. Ch.: Adam
P., 1893; Arthur[6], 1888.

559.

Elizabeth[5] C. Hovis (Jacob[4], &c.), m. Charles Keesey, hotel
k. York, Pa. Luth. Ch.: (560) Jennie[6], 1865, m.
D. A. Minnich, postmaster, York, Pa. Luth. Ch.:
Earl, 1886, and Grace, 1888; (561) Percy[6], 1870.
Luth., m. Almond Bitner. Ch.: Herman, Keturah,
Charles; (562) Minnie[6], 1874, m. John Beigh. Ch.: 0.

568.

ELIZABETH[4] HOVIS (Barbara[3], Felix, &c.), m. Jacob
Shaffer, d. 1866. Farm. Luth. Ch.: 10: Sarah[5] A.,
1845–1886; (569) Barbara[5], 1846; (571) Lucy[5] A.,
1847; (576) Elizabeth[5], 1850; (578) William[5], 1852.
Farm. Luth. Winterstown, Pa., m. Rachel Dietz.
Ch.: Nacie, 1886, and William J., 1892; Josiah[5], 1854–

1854; Melvina[5], 1856-1887; (579) Caroline[6], 1858, m.
Jeremiah Lentz. Farm. Jacobus, Pa. Luth. Ch.:
Elmer, 1882; Carrie, 1885; Jennie, 1887; Jacob[5], 1860-
1860; (580) Emanuel[5], 1862, m. Ida Stine. Farm.
Tilton, Pa. Luth. Ch.: Blanche, 1887, Macleda, 1890;
Christian, 1899.

569.

Barbara[5] Shaffer (Elizabeth[4], Barbara[3], &c.), m. Samuel
Rider, c. box mnf., Tilton, Pa. Luth. Ch.: Ida[6], 1871;
Alpheus[6], 1873-1892; (570) Mary[6], 1877, m. Chas. Gin-
gerich. Ch.: Lester; Harry, 1881; Bertha, 1886.

571.

Lucy[5] A. Shaffer (Elizabeth[4], &c.), m. Henry Grothe, farm.
Jacobus, Pa. Luth. Ch.: (572) William[6] E., 1870;
(573) Chas.[6] A., 1872. Luth. m. Ellen Wambaugh.
Ch.: Greda[6] M., 1894; (574) Clara[6] M., 1874; (575)
Mary[6] E., 1875; Samuel[6] T., 1877-1877.

572.

William[6] E. Grothe (Lucy[5] A., Elizabeth[4], &c.), lab. Luth.
m. Alice Sippel. Ch.: Harry, 1891; William, 1893;
Virginia M., 1895; Mabel.

574.

Clara[6] M. Grothe (Lucy[5] A., &c.), m. Edward Richard.
Luth. Ch.: Harry G., 1889; Chas. A., 1891; Elsie M.,
1894; Lucy A., 1896-1896; Lizzie E., 1896-1898.

575.

Mary[6] E. Grothe (Lucy[5] A., &c.), m. William Sprenkle.
Ch.: Roy G., 1894; Edward B., 1896; John H., 1898.

576.

Elizabeth[5] Shaffer (Elizabeth[4], Barbara[3], &c.), m. Albert
Geiselman, farm., Jacobus, Pa. U. B. Ch.: William
H., 1876; (577) William, m. Cora Leader. Cig. m.
Jacobus, Pa. Ch.: One, inft.

581.

JESSE[4] HOVIS (Barbara[3], Felix, &c.), m. 1st, Catharine
Wart; m. 2nd, Matilda Sprenkle. Ch.: (582) Amanda[5]
C., 1852–1896, m. George Linebaugh, Spry, Pa. Ch.:
Eddie, 1872; William, d. inf.; Charles, 1880; (583)
Anna[5], 1868–1894, m. Albert Winega, Spry, Pa. Luth.
Ch.: Lillie, 1880; William[5], 1855–1862; (584) Frank-
lin[5], m. Lizzie Winega. Farm, Spry, Pa. Luth. Ch.:
Kerwin, 1885, and Lollie, 1887; (585) Albert[5], 1866,
farm. Luth. Spry, Pa. m. Maggie Grim. Ch.:
Spurgeon, 1888; (586) Lydia[5], 1869, m. John Strewig,
farm. Luth. Spry, Pa. Ch.: Mamie, 1888, and Perry
1884; Charles[5], 1872.

587.

FRANKLIN[4] HOVIS (Barbara[3], Felix, &c.), m. Leah Morri-
son. Farm. Luth. Ch.: 11: Melvina[5], 1851–1852;
(588) Mahala[5], 1853, m. Jacob Dietz. Ch.: 2, both d.
infts.; Reuben[5], 1854–1856; (589) Samuel[5], 1856; inft.
son[5], d.; Mary[5] J., 1858–1861; (590) Henrietta[5], 1860;
(591) Franklin[5], 1865, m. Sarah Strewig. Farm. Luth.
Ch.: Mabel J., 1893; Ralph E., 1897; Cora M.; 1899;
(592) Sarah[5] A., 1867, m. Clinton Ness, railroader, Luth.
Ch.: Helen M., 1885–1886; Wilbert, 1899; (593)
Jacob[5], 1869; an inft. son[5], d.

589.

Samuel[5] Hovis (Franklin[4], Barbara[3], &c.), m. Sarah Landis.
Farm. Luth. Ch.: Harry, 1881; Arthur, 1891; James
F., 1886–1886; Clarence J., 1885–1892; inft. son,
1879, d.

590.

Henrietta[5] Hovis (Franklin[4], &c.), m. George King, farm.
Luth. Ch.: Sadie A., 1883–1883; Elmer B., 1886;
Leah M., 1890; Maggie M., 1892–1897; Raymond F.,
1898.

593.

Jacob⁵ Hovis (Franklin⁴, &c.), m. Martha McDole. Farm. Luth. Ch.: Mary J., 1893–1896; Emma G., 1896; Elizabeth E., 1898; Franklin J., 1900.

CHAPTER 13TH.— MARGARETTA.

594.

MARGARETTA³ GLATFELTER (Felix², Casper¹), b. May 12th, 1784, d. Apr. 16, 1856, buried at Shrewsbury, Pa., m. Philip Folckommer, farm. Luth. Res. near Shrewsbury. Ch.: 11, b. between 1805–1835. (595) Henry; (598) Jacob; (604) Barbara; (605) Margaretta; m. Mr. Lowe, West Milton, Ohio. Ch.: Henry and others unk.; (605a) William, m. to un. Res. Lafayette, Ind. Ch.: un.; (606) Jonathan, m. Louisa Fry. Res. Canton, Ohio. Ch.: Anna and others; (607) Elizabeth; (611) John, m. to un. Res. Covington, Ohio. Ch.: Leonidas, Aubrey, Mary; (612) Daniel, m. Julia Miller. Res. Shrewsbury, Pa. Ch.: John, William, Mary, Emma; (613) Charles, m. to un. Res. West Milton, Ohio. Ch.: one daughter; (614) Mary, m. Levi Ruhl. Res. Springfield, Ohio. Ch.: Josiah, Albertus, May, Margaret.

595.

HENRY⁴ FOLCKOMER (Margaretta³, Felix, &c.), m. Kate Sewensel. Res. Shrewsbury, Pa. Ch. of 1st wife: (596) Margaret, m. Henry Bailey, d., res. Baltimore, Md.; (597) Susan, m. Israel Blain, res. New Oxford, Pa.; Frank, res. Covington, Ohio; Samuel, Springfield, Ohio; Henry, Quincy, Ill.; Oliver, d., Ohio; Ch. of 3d wife: (Jane Gordon) Clara; Williamsa, res. Baltimore, Md.; Chester, Quincy, Ill.; Eliza; Willias, d.; 2d wife was Agnes J. Gordon. Ch.: 0.

598.

JACOB[4] FOLCKOMER (Margaretta[3], &c.), m. Susan Boyer.
Res. Shrewsbury, Pa.   Ch. : 9 : (599) Rebecca[5], m. Geo.
W. Blasser; Samuel[5], d.; (600) Mary[5], m. William H.
Smyser; Susan[5]; (601) George[5] W., m. Emma Klinefel-
ter; (602) Isaac[5], d., m. Mary E. Klinefelter; Sarah[5] E.,
res. Baltimore, Md. ; (603) Jacob[6], m. Mary Dinteman.
Res. Stewartstown, Pa.; Ellen[5], d. at 5 yrs.

604.

BARBARA[4] FOLCKOMER (Margaretta[3], &c.), m. Geo. Filbey, West Milton, Ohio.   Ch. : Oliver, George, Frank,
Joseph, Elleana, d. ; Rebecca, Margaret.

607.

ELIZABETH[4] FOLCKOMER (Margaretta[3], &c.), m. Abraham Sechrist. Shrewsbury, Pa. Ch.: (608) Henrietta[5],
d., m. Frank Gosnell; (609) Charles[5], d., m. Julia Klinefelter. Ch.: John, Leora, Anna ; (610) Mary[5], d., m.
Thomas McAkee; John[5], d. ; Anna[5], d.

Chapter 14th.— CASPER.

615.

CASPER[3] GLATFELTER (Felix[2], Casper[1]), m. Mary
Emig. Moved West about 1825, settling near Springfield, Ohio. Ch.: William to Iowa; (616) John Peter,
1812–1865; (615a) Charles to Missouri; Leah; Rachel;
Katy, and several others, names unk.; (615b) Rachel,
m. Mr. Killdow. Two died at Marshall, Ill.

616.

JOHN[4] P. GLATFELTER (Casper[3], Felix[2], &c.), m. Louisa
Smith. Left Ohio, returned to York co., Pa., rearing
a family of 12 children. Carp. Luth. Ch.: (617)

William S., 1841; (617a) Henrietta, 1842–1866; (618)
Lydia, 1844; Franklin, 1846–1848; David, 1848–1866;
(621) Matilda, 1849; (623) Selinda[5], 1852–1883, m.
Franklin Welsh, lab. Luth. Ch.: (624) George[6], who
m. Mae Blank; Jacob P., 1848, unm., Springfield, Ohio;
James B., 1856–1866; Charles V., died a year after re-
lease from Andersonville prison; (624a) John C., 1859,
m. 1st, Lulu Bortner, 2nd, Katy Shatler. Luth. Ch.:
Reyburn B., and John C., 1884; (625) George[5] W.,
1862. Ch.: 3 dead, 4 living; (626) Sophia[5].

617.

William[5] S. Glatfelter (John[4] P., Casper[3], &c.), m. A. C.
Lankenau. Contractor, Springfield, Ohio. Luth. Ch.:
Charles F., 1871, who fills an important position as clerk
in Chicago.

618.

Lydia[5] Glatfelter (John[4] P., &c.), m. Franklin Stambaugh,
farm. Luth. Ch.: (619) Luther[6], 1868, m. Sarah Wier.
Ch.: One; (620) Sarah[6], 1870, m. Charles Welsh;
William[6].

621.

Matilda[5] Glatfelter (John[4] P., &c.), m. Emanuel Richkrick, a
miller. Luth. Ch.: (622) Emma[6] C., 1872, m. Charles
Emig. Luth. Ch.: Violetta, 1892, Walter, 1893, Raymond, inft.

626.

Sophia[5] Glatfelter (John P., &c.), m. Wm. Shriver, farm.
Luth. Res. near Brillhart Sta. Ch.: (627) Clara[6] E.,
1861, m. Ephraim Rohrbaugh, railroader. Luth. Ch.:
12; (628) Wit[6] H., m. Ellen Huben. Ch.: 3; (629)
Hattie[6] A., m. David Shindler.

617a.

Henrietta[5] Glatfelter (John[4] P., Casper[3], &c.), m. Mr. Falkenstine. Ch.: 0. Luth.

PART III. — CASPER², AND DESCENDANTS.

631.

CASPER² GLATFELTER (Casper¹). We have already noted Casper as a Revolutionary soldier. A part of the old Philip Glatfelter farm, Codorus twp., was covered by two warrants in the name of Casper, dated April 3d, 1770, and Oct. 4th, 1771. Our knowledge of his descendants is quite incomplete. His children were (632) Charles, Eva, Adam, Rosanna; (677) Jacob; (636) John; (635) Joseph; (659) Casper.

EVA³ and ADAM³, d. young, unm.; (634) ROSANNA³, m. Mr. Boyer, moved to Ohio. Ch.: 4; (635) JOSEPH³ had one son, Joseph A. ("Little Joey,") d. unm. 1898, aet. 76 yrs.

632.

CHARLES³ GLATFELTER (Casper², Casper¹), moved to Indiana. He had a son (633) Levi, who moved to and d. at Caney, Kans. Ch.: 9: George, Casper, Charles, at same place, and Cleam, res. un.; 2 dau., res. I. T.; 2 sons and 1 dau., d.

CHAPTER 15TH. — JOHN.

636.

JOHN³ GLATFELTER (Casper², Casper¹). Farmer. Res. in the latter years of his life at the foot of "Dunker Valley," Springfield twp., York co., Pa. Ch.: (637) Isaac K.,

1825–1895 ; (648) John, 1820 ; (651) Samuel, 1819–1866 ;
(658) Juliann.

637.

ISAAC[4] K. GLATFELTER (John[3], Casper[2], &c.), m. Sarah
Feiser. Farm., res. Springfield twp. Widow lives now
at York, Pa. Ch.: 9: (638) Anna M., 1850; (640)
Isaac J., 1852; (641) Frank P., 1854; (643) John K.,
1855 ; (644) Samuel F., 1858; Sarah E., 1863; (645)
Emma C., 1865 ; (646) Louisa J., 1869; (647) David
L., 1873.

638.

Anna[5] M. Glatfelter (Isaac[4], John[3], &c.), m. Abdiel Bortner,
York, Pa. Ch.: a son, Franklin M., 1873, (639) m.
Bertha Crider.

640.

Isaac[5] J. Glatfelter (Isaac[4], &c.), m. Emma E. Julius. Pro-
duce commission dealer, York, Pa. Luth. Ch.: 0.

641.

Franklin[5] P. Glatfelter (Isaac[4], &c.), m. Eliza Fahringer.
Farm. and lumber dealer. Res. Jacobus, Pa. Pref.
Luth. Ch.: (642) Emma[6], 1879, m. Jesse Williams,
Glen Rock. Ch.: Frank G.; Elsie[6] A., 1882; Grover[6]
A., 1892.

643.

John[5] K. Glatfelter (Isaac[4], &c.), m. Mary Flinchbaugh.
Lab. York, Pa. Luth.: Ch.: Mamie V., 1888, and
Beulah M. E., 1890.

644.

Samuel[5] F. Glatfelter (Isaac[4], &c.) m. Ida A. Gilbert. Contractor and builder, York, Pa. Evang. Ch.: 0.

645.

Emma C[5]. Glatfelter (Isaac[4], &c.), m. Charles W. Yeatts, milk
traffic, York, Pa. U. B. Ch.: Earl R., 1894, and Stewart McK., 1895.

646.

Louisa[5] J. Glatfelter (Isaac[4], &c.), m. Allen H. Henise, book k., York, Pa. U. B. Ch.: Paul G., 1897, and Sarah L., 1894.

647.

David[5] L. Glatfelter (Isaac[4], &c.), m. Anna L.——. Bankteller, Columbia, Pa. Presb. Ch.: David, 1895; Frank, 1896; Sarah, 1899.

648.

JOHN[4] GLATFELTER (John[3], Casper[2], &c.), had 10 children, 6 d. in infancy. The living are: (649) Isaac[5], 1848, m. Maggie Southworth. Res. Glen Rock, Pa. Ref. Ch.: Maud B., 1887, and Sarah J., 1885; Samuel[5], unm. York, Pa.; Mary[5], unm. Jacobus, Pa.; (650) Havana[5], m., res. Phila., Pa.

651.

SAMUEL[4] GLATFELTER, d. (John[3], &c.), farm. near York, Pa. Luth. Ch.: 8: (652) Susan[5], 1845–1895; (653) Julian[5], 1846, m. Levi Bentzel, Stehley, Pa. Ch.: 0; (654) Margaret[5] E., 1847, m. Jacob LeCrone, Weigelstown, Pa. Ch.: Charles, Samuel, Harry, John, and 4 d. infts.; (655) Amanda[5] J., 1850–1883, m. Peter S. LeCrone, York, Pa. Ch.: Samuel L. and Rebecca J.; Catharine[5], 1848–1870, unm.; (656) Isabella[5], 1857–1877, m. Peter F. LeCrone, Emigsville, Pa. Ch.: Peter F. and Howard C.; (657) Emma[5] L., 1857–1887, m. North A. Wire. Ch.: 0.; Samuel[5] L., 1854–1879, unm.

652.

Susan[5] Glatfelter (Samuel[4], John[3], &c.), m. Jacob Rebman, York, Pa. Ch.: Amanda E., Peter F., Edward C., Albert, Kate, Ella, Sallie, Edna, John, Paul.

658.

JULIAN[4] GLATFELTER (John[3], Casper[2], &c.), m. Matthias Schwer, farm. Luth. Ch.: Clinton, 1849, Res. Scranton, Pa.; Elizabeth, 1861, unm. York, Pa.

Chapter 16th. — CASPER.

659.

CASPER³ GLATFELTER, 1797–1869 (Casper², Casper¹),
m. Elizabeth Sulsbach who d. 1887, aet. 86 yrs. Ch.:
9: (660) Jacob S.; (664) Frederick, (d.), 1844; (667)
Casper; (668) George, 1832–1898; (672) John to Ohio.
Ch.: 4; (673) David; Magdalena, m. Henry Forscht
(see No. 231); (674) Susan, 1840; (675) Anna.

660.

JACOB⁴ S. GLATFELTER (Casper³, &c.), m. Caroline
Sprenkle. Sta. engineer, York, Pa. Luth. Ch.; (661)
Calvin, 1861; (662) Harry, 1862; Emma, 1864; Sarah,
1866; (663) Reuben, 1867, m. Phoebe Tinsley. Res.
N. York City. Ch.: Blanche, d.; Clara⁵, 1875.

661.

Calvin⁵ Glatfelter (Jacob⁴ S., Casper³, &c.), m. Euphemia
Shetter. Res. Wrightsville, Pa. Blacksmith. Ch.: 0.

662.

Harry⁵ Glatfelter (Jacob⁴ S., &c.), m. Catharine Daly. Cig.
m. Springfield, Mass. Unaf. Ch.: Henry, 1887;
Edmund C., 1880–1893; Russel L., 1892; Ralph J.,
1896, Helen C., 1898.

664.

FREDERICK⁴ GLADFELTER (Casper³, Casper², &c.), m.
Julian Barre. Farmer, Princeville, Ill. Unaf. Ch.:
(665) Lizzie A., 1869; m. to un. Ch.: son and daughter; Jonas, 1871; Minnie M., 1874; (666) Bessie A.,
1875; Casper L., 1879; Alice B., 1880; Retta G., 1882;
Logan B., 1884.

666.

Bessie[5] A. Gladfelter (Frederick[4], Casper[3], &c.), m. Albert Peterson. Ch.: Glenn, 1896–1896, Roscoe, 1897; Alia, 1899.

667.

CASPER[4] GLATFELTER (Casper[3], Casper[2] &c.), m. Juretta G. Hare. Farm. Havana, Kans. Unaf. Ch.: 0.

668.

GEORGE[4] GLADFELTER, d. (Casper[3], &c.), m. 3d wife, Eliza Hammer. Res. Princeville, Ill. Ch.: Helen, 1846; Albert, 1848; (669) George, 1850; Elizabeth, 1852; Henry, 1853; Frederick, 1854; Jacob, 1855; (670) Madelina, 1857; m. Thos. Gill, Peoria, Ill. Ch.: 0; Daniel, 1858; Eliza, 1860; (671) Casper, 1862, m. Maggie Whitehead. Ch.: William.

669.

George[5] Gladfelter (George[4], Casper[3], &c.) m. Emma Deboard. Res. Princeville, Ill. Ch.: Lloyd, Bertha and Nellie.

672.

JOHN[4] GLATFELTER (Casper[3], Casper[2], &c.), died at Springfield, Ohio. Ch.: 4: Leah, Annie, Henry and John. Leah lives in Dayton, Ohio; Annie in Springfield, Ohio; Henry was killed, 1874; John lives in Michigan.

673.

DAVID[4] GLADFELTER (Casper[3], &c.), was m., lived at Princeville, Ill., died a soldier in hospital during Civil War. Widow res. at Emporia, Kans. Ch.: 2.

674.

SUSAN[4] GLADFELTER (Casper[3], &c.), m. Geo. Tarbox, shoemaker, Princeville, Ill. Unaf. Ch.: 0.

675.

ANNA[4] GLADFELTER (Casper[3], &c.), died 5 yrs. ago, was married to Henry Haag, Havana, Kans., farm. Presb. Ch.: Francis, 1855; (676) Henry G., 1864, m. Nettie M. Pritchard. Ch.: One, George P., 1891; and 8 others dead.

CHAPTER 17TH. — JACOB.

677.

JACOB[3] GLATFELTER (Casper[2], Casper[1]), moved to Clinton co., Pa. Ch.: 10: (678) Jacob; (679) Jesse; (680) Elizabeth; (681) Mary; (682) Lydia; (685a) Sarah, m. Silas Kester. Res. What Cheer, Iowa. Ch.: 0; and 4 names unk.

678.

JACOB[4] GLATFELTER (Jacob[3], Casper[2], &c.), m. 1st, Mary Gipe. Ch.: William, Julia, Wesley, Mary; m. 2d, Elizabeth Pasel. Ch.: Samuel, Ellen, John and Jacob.

679.

JESSE[4] GLATFELTER (Jacob[3], &c.), m. 1st, Hannah Kester. Ch.: John, Elizabeth, Franklin, Nancy, Calvin, Esther, Elmer, Elijah; m. 2d, to Esther, sister of 1st wife.

680.

ELIZABETH[4] GLATFELTER (Jacob[3], &c.), m. Abraham Pittenger. Ch.: Jacob, William, Margaret, Mary, Sarah, Annie, Samuel.

681.

MARY[4] GLATFELTER (Jacob[3], &c.), m. Andrew Kettner, Van Cleave, Iowa. Ch.: Jane, Mary, Elmira, Frances, Catherine, Richard, Adam.

682.

LYDIA[4] GLATFELTER (Jacob[3], &c.), m. Henry Henderson.
Ch.: William; (683) Emily; (685) Mary, m. John
Fellmalee, Sebatha, Kans; Charlotte.

683.

Emily[5] Henderson (Lydia[4], Jacob[3], &c.), m. William Rhine,
Tylersville, Pa. Ch.: Eliza[6] (684) m. Murray Banks,
Wallacton, Pa. Ch.: Lizzie[7]; Henry[6], Mary[6], Harry[6],
Albert[6].

Part IV. — HENRY, AND HIS DESCENDANTS.

685b.

HENRY[2] GLATFELTER (Casper[1]), m. Margaret,
daughter of John Heilman, original owner of the tract on
which Okete is located. He introduced the " Heilman
pear " from Germany. Henry was probably the youngest
of Casper's sons. Farmer. A deed made 1834 in the possession of Andrew B. Glatfelter, grandson of Henry, notes
that by reason of a will made by Henry, 1833, 125 acres in
Codorus twp. is conveyed to his son Jacob, and further
notes that this was part of a tract conveyed from Michael
Heilman to Henry Glatfelter, April 10th, 1802; that the
same was originally entered by warrant by Felix Miller,
1746. The reason those first comers settled in the hilly
parts rather than in the richer limestone valleys, is said
to have been, the natural springs of water; also the
quicker and surer growth of rye. Henry's children were:
(686) Michael, (700) Philip, (701) Jacob, (767) Harry,
(800) Frederick, (801) Amelia, (728) Daniel.

(700) **PHILIP**[3], moved to Juniatta co., Pa., some 60 years ago. He had 8 children. Have not been able to secure further knowledge of his family. (800) **FREDERICK**[3] died about 50 years ago at Okete, Pa. He had 6 or 7 children. A son, Solomon, is said to live in Lancaster, Ohio; a daughter in Baltimore, Md. (801) **AMELIA**[3] was married to Mr. Hosler, had 3 children, Jacob, Harry and Catharine, all dead.

CHAPTER 18TH. — MICHAEL.

686.

MICHAEL[3] **GLATFELTER** (Henry[2], Casper[1]), d. 1821. Ch.: (687) Caroline; (688) Ephraim B., 1836; (698) Sarah R.; (699) Matilda.

687.

CAROLINE[4] GLATFELTER (Michael[3], Henry[2], &c.), m. David Lepo. Ch.: Josiah, Michael, Mary A., Lizzie, Sarah A., Jacob.

688.

EPHRAIM[4] B. GLATFELTER (Michael[3], &c.), m. Catharine Hamm. Farm. near Okete. Luth. Ch.: 12: (689) Elizabeth[5], 1857; (691) Sylvester[5] D., 1859; (693) Michael[5], 1862; (694) Kate[5], m. Geo. Gentzler, Seven-valley. Ch.: Howard J. and Beatrice; (695) Lydiann[5], 1857; (696) Susan[5], 1874, m. Samuel Klinedinst, N. York, Pa. Office cl. Ch.: 0; (696a) Ellen[5], 1879, m. Daniel Emenhiser, c. m., N. York, Pa. Ch.: Harry J. and Rosie B.; (697) Ephraim[5], 1876; Harvey[5] J., 1881; Rosie[5] B., 1883; Peter[5] and Eli[5], d.

689.

Elizabeth[5] Glatfelter (Ephraim[4], Michael[3], &c.), m. John A. Sheffer, Vet. Surg., Okete, Pa. Luth. Ch.: (690)

Bert A., 1878, m. Sallie Ramble. Teacher. Ch.:
Helen[7] G., d., and John[7] A.; Carrie V., 1880; Sarah K.,
1882; John E., 1883; Ephraim C., 1885; Geo. E.,
1889; Elsie N., 1890; Ralph E., 1892; Clarence E.,
1894; Earl E., 1897.

691.

Sylvester[6] D. Glatfelter (Ephraim[4], Michael[3], &c.) m. Louisa
Martin. Res. Bair Sta., Pa. c. m. Luth. Ch.: 5;
(692) Bessie A., 1878, m. Bertram Richards, Bair Sta.,
supt. c. mnf. Ch.: 0; Albert T., 1880; Sadie E., 1883;
Martin C., 1885–1886; Ernest S., 1893.

693.

Michael[5] Glatfelter (Ephraim[4], &c.), m. Martha J. Brenneman. Vet. Surg. Jacobus, Pa. Luth. Ch.: Herman
E., 1884; Vertie J., 1891; Guy V., 1893; Fairie W.,
1898.

695.

Lydiann[5] Glatfelter (Ephraim[4], &c.), m. Winfield Hildebrand.
Bair Sta., Pa. c. m. Luth. Ch.: Sophia L., 1888;
Ada M., 1890; Charles W., 1896.

697.

Ephraim[5] Glatfelter (Ephraim[4], &c.), m. Sadie M. Gentzler.
Res., N. York, Pa. c. m. Luth. Ch.: Fairie E.,
1896–1898; Laurence W., 1899.

698.

SARAH[4] GLATFELTER (Michael[3], Henry, &c.), m. Michael
Emig. Ch.: Michael, Charles, Louisa.

699.

MATILDA[4] GLATFELTER (Michael[3], &c.), m. Michael
Krout. Ch.: Emeline, Mary A., Caroline, Lizzie,
Matilda, Jane, Isabel.

CHAPTER 19TH.— JACOB.

701.

JACOB[3] GLATFELTER (Henry[2], Casper[1]). Farm. at Okote, Pa. Ch.: (702) Cordelia; Lavina, d. unm.; (707) David B., 1832; (711) Henry B., 1835; (719) Jacob B., 1836; (723) Andrew B., 1837; (724) Rudolph B., 1847; (725) Leah; Michael, Mary, George and Hezekiah, all d. young; Louisa, unm.

702.

CORDELIA[4] GLATFELTER (Jacob[3], Henry[2], &c.), m. Michael Klinedinst. Ch.: Franklin P., unm.: Charles, unm.; (703) Martha J.; Mollie, unm.; (704) Michael G., m. Annie Grim. Ch.: 2.; (705) Hattie, m. J. S. Bair; (706) Sallie, m. John E. Gentzler. Ch.: 2; Leah, unm.

703.

Martha[5] J. Klinedinst (Cordelia[4], Jacob[3], &c.), m. John Baukert. Ch.: Jennie, Orphie, Ezra, Macie, Herschel, Jairous, Edwin, Regina.

707.

DAVID[4] B. GLATFELTER (Jacob[3], &c.), m. Emeline[5] J. Glatfelter (Jesse, Philip, Felix, &c.). Retired farm. Ref. Brillhart Sta. Ch.: (708) Rosie P., 1866; (709) David G., 1871; (710) Phoebe N., 1873; Jacob G., 1879, a teacher; Chauncey G., 1886.

708.

Rosie[5] P. Glatfelter (David[4] B., Jacob[3], &c.), m. Henry Boyer, farm. Jacobus, Pa. Ch.: Harry, 1886; Beulah, 1890.

709.

David[5] G. Glatfelter (David[4] B., &c.), m. Clara Bupp. Ch.: Walter, 1893; Mark, 1895; Jessie M., 1897.

710.

Phoebe⁵ N. Glatfelter (David⁴ B., &c.) m. Charles Hershey, Spring Forge. Merch. Luth. Wife, ref. Ch.: Florence E., 1896; Effie E., 1897; Lester G., 1899.

711.

HENRY⁴ B. GLATFELTER, d. (Jacob³, Henry², &c.), m. Ellen Klinedinst. Widow, res. in N. York, Pa. Ref. Ch.: 18: Ida J., 1864–1869; (712) Jacob W., 1868–1893; (713) Rudolph Z., 1869; Sarah A., 1870–1881; (714) Frederick M., 1873; Ellen, 1874–1874; (715) Henry K., 1875; (716) Hallie J., m. Harry Free. Ch.: Bessie⁶, 1897; George C., 1878–1878; Percy B., 1881–1891; Jay, 1887–1888; Ray, 1887–1887; Lottie S., 1884; Gertrude A., 1887; Ray S., 1889–1890; Guy E., 1891–1891; (717) Andrew D., 1878; (718) Kate V. m., Geo. Ketterman, c. m. N. York. Ch.: Ellen, d. inft., and Ray.

712.

Jacob⁵ W. Gladfelter (Henry⁴ B., Jacob³, &c.), m. to un. Ch.: Mabel B., Irwin, Ralph A., Florence, d.

713.

Rudy⁵ Z. Gladfelter (Henry⁴ B., Jacob³, &c.), m. Kittie V. Senft. Cig. pack. N. York, Pa. Ref. Ch.: Curtis S., 1882; Ada B., 1892; Flora E., 1894; John H., 1897; Ray S., 1899.

714.

Frederick⁵ M. Gladfelter (Henry⁴ B., &c.), m. Mary Gunnet. C. m. at Okete, Pa. Ref. Ch.: Violet J., 1893; Earl B., 1896; Lucy E., 1897; Lottie.

715.

Henry⁵ K. Gladfelter (Henry⁴ B., &c.), m. Lucy Seneft. C. m. N. York, Pa. Ref. Ch.: Guy E., 1895; Helen J., 1897; Mary E., 1899.

717.

Andrew[5] D. Glatfelter (Henry[4] B., &c.), m. Mary E. Gilbert. Cig. dealer. N. York, Pa. Ref. Ch.: Nellie F., 1899.

719.

JACOB[4] B. GLATFELTER (Jacob[3], Henry[2]), m. Lucinda Hamm. Res. Okete, Pa. Farm. Ref. Ch.: (720) Lillie S., 1865; Daniel R., 1867–1871; (721) Jacob A., 1870; (722) Rosie V., 1872.

720.

Lillie[5] S. Glatfelter (Jacob[4] B., Jacob[3], &c.), m. A. P. Gunnet, carp. Okete. Ch.: Lottie I.; Margaret R., Ursinus L.; Mary L.; William.

721.

Jacob[5] A. Glatfelter (Jacob[4] B., &c.), m. Minnie Laub. Res. Okete. Lab. at paper mill. Ref. Ch.: Willis S., 1890; Ralph C., 1891; Esther R., 1894; Edward A., 1896; Herman J., 1898; Goldie C., 1900.

722.

Rosie[5] V. Glatfelter (Jacob[4] B., &c.), m. Lee S. Fake, teacher at Okete, Pa. Ch.: Francis L., Thos. J., Sudie M., Myra V., Bessie E., James L.

723.

ANDREW[4] B. GLATFELTER (Jacob[3], Henry[2], &c.), m. Sarah N. Walker. Res. Okete. Farm. Ref. Ch.: 0.

724.

RUDOLPH[4] B. GLATFELTER (Jacob[3], &c.), m. Rosa Hamm. Res. East Berlin, Adams co., Pa. Ch.: Percy, a teacher; Ursinus L., 1877; Lydia, 1880; Annie M. E., 1882.

725.

LEAH[4] GLATFELTER (Jacob[3], &c.), m. Geo. Myer, York,
Pa. Ch.: (726) Andrew[5], res. Okete, m. Miss Bentz.
Ch.: 2; (727) Annie[5], m. Mr. Starbach. Ch.: 3; (728)
Leah[5], m. Wm. Zink. Ch. 2; George[5], d. young;
Naomi[5], unm.

CHAPTER 20TH. — DANIEL.

728.

DANIEL[3] GLATFELTER (Henry[2], Casper[1]), m. Katy
Kling, of English descent. He died, aged 86; wife d.
at 75. Farmer and distiller, Manchester twp. Ref.
Ch.: 10: (729) Rebecca; (743) Eliza, 1822; (750)
Susan; Mattie; (751) John, 1827; (755) Henry, d.
1832; (757) Sarah A.; (760) Melvina; (765) Daniel;
Leah, d. young.

729.

REBECCA[4] GLATFELTER (Daniel[3], Henry[2], &c.), m.
Henry Miller, d. Ch.: (730) Charles W., 1840; (734)
Emeline, 1841; m. Mr. Wagner; (735) Louisa, 1843;
(740) Theodore, 1845; John, 1847; (742a) Gustave,
1849; (742b) Daniel, 1851; George, 1854; (742c)
William, 1856; (742) Edward P., 1861.

730.

Charles[5] W. Miller (Rebecca[4], Daniel[3], &c.). Farm. Allens-
ville, Vinton Co., Ohio. Meth. Ch.: (731) Amanda
J., 1860, m. James Hartley; Lydia E., 1869; (732)
Sarah E., 1872, m. A. M. Johnson; (733) Emma L.,
1875, m. D. C. Turner; Henry C., 1879; William F.,
1882; Ida M., 1884; Charles C., 1889.

735.

Louisa[5] Miller (Rebecca[4], &c.), m. John H. Freed, Abbottstown, Pa. Luth. Ch.: 12: (736) Elmer[6] E., 1864–1893; Geo.[6] W., 1861; (737) Grant[6], 1865; m. Anne Fissel, Abbottstown, Pa. Ch.: Cora M., 1898; Henry[6] C., 1867–1869; (738) Daniel[6] W., 1869, m. Amanda Hale. Res. Jacob's Mills, Pa. Ch.: Mabel M., 1890; Agnes[6] A., 1872–1872; Ida[6] M., 1874; (739) Emma[6] R., 1876, m. Allen Myers, Hanover, Pa. Ch.: Irene F., 1898, and Gladys M., 1900; Harvey[6] E., 1879; J. Willis[6], 1881; Chas.[6] C., 1884; Cora[6] A., 1885.

736.

Elmer[6] E. Freed (Louisa[5], Rebecca[4], &c.), m. Jane Witters. Res. New Oxford, Pa. Ch.: Bertha G., 1888; Clare, 1890; J. Nevin, 1892.

740.

Theodore[5] Miller (Rebecca[4], Daniel[3], &c.), m. Sarah Nagle. Lab. York, Pa. Luth. Ch.: (741) Dara, 1870, m. John D. Berkheimer; Winfield, 1872–1874; Minnie, 1875; Annie, 1880.

742.

Edward[5] P. Miller (Rebecca[4], &c.), m. Miriam J. Baker. Merch. Abbottstown, Pa. Luth. Ch.: Harriet R., 1890; Geo. E., 1892.

742a.

Gustave[5] Miller (Rebecca[4], &c.), b. 1849, m. Jennie Miller. Railroader. Luth. Abbottstown, Pa. Ch.: Roy E., 1887; Rebecca S., 1892; Edward L., 1892.

742b.

Daniel[5] Miller (Rebecca[4], &c.), 1851, m. Mary E. ——. Hotel-keeper. Luth. Abbottstown, Pa. Ch.: William, 1876–1876; Annie M., 1878; Henry E., 1880; Herman, 1885.

742c.

William[5] Miller (Rebecca[4], &c.), b. 1856, m. Alice ——.
Railroader. Abbottstown, Pa. Luth. Ch.: Harry A.,
1878; Henry C., 1879; Chas. E., 1881; William R.,
1884; Margarete, 1888; Rachel, 1891. Harry is married.

743.

ELIZA[4] GLATFELTER (Daniel[3], Henry[2], &c.), m. 1st,
Henry Wolf (d.) Ch.: (744) Henry, 1840; (745)
John P., 1844–1899; (746) Catharine, 1846; (749a)
William, 1849–1899, m. Susan Geise, res. N. Codorus.
Ch.: 5; (749b) Michael, 1852, m. Ellen Genzler. Res.
W. Manchester twp. Ch: 4; (749c) Daniel, 1855, m.
Amelia Genzler. Res. York, Pa. Ch.: 4. 2nd, m.
Israel Fishel (d.). Widow res. at N. Salem, Pa. Ch.:
one; (749d) Israel, 1860, m. Lucy A. Ruhl. Res. N.
Salem. Teacher. Ref. Ch.: 4.

744.

Henry[5] Wolf (Eliza[4], Daniel[3], &c.), m. Margaret A. Wolf.
Res. York, Pa. Ch.: Robert, Curtin, Edward, Thomas,
Sallie, Sarah, Maggie.

745.

John[5] P. Wolf (Eliza[4], &c.), m. Lizzie Smyser. Res. Glen
Rock, Pa. Ch.: Jacob and Ida.

746.

Catharine[5] Wolf (Eliza[4], &c.), m. Nathan Folckomer, N.
Salem. Ch.: 9: (747) H. Spangler[6], m. Jennie Kopp.
Res. N. Salem. Ch.: 3; (748) James[6], m. Sarah
Eyster. Res. N. Codorus. Ch.: 4; (749) Meda[6], m.
Mr. Brenneman, Old Codorus. Ch.: a number; Ro-
man[6], Sadie[6], Arch[6], Nathan[6], Paul[6], Harry[6].

750.

SUSAN[4] GLATFELTER (Daniel[3], Henry[2], &c.), m. 1st,
Emanuel Ramer. Died in Ill. Ch.: 0; m. 2d, Paul
Moyer. Ch.: 0.

751.

JOHN[4] GLATFELTER (Daniel[3], Henry[2], &c.), m. Melinda
Messersmith. Farm, at N. Salem, Pa. Ref. Ch.: (752)
Albert M., 1859; (753) Mary E., 1862; (754) Catherine
M., 1866; Jennie M., 1877, unm., a dressmaker.

752.

Albert[5] M. Glatfelter (John[4], Daniel[3], &c.), m. Kate Aughen-
baugh. Res. N. Salem. Farm. Ch.: William E.,
1883; Ada M., 1889; Annie M., 1891; Alda M., 1898.

753.

Mary[5] E. Glatfelter (John[4], &c.), m. John A. Eyster, farm.,
near Okete, Pa. Ch.: John E., Ada M., Erwin, Francis,
Seymour, Elizabeth, Paris, Miller, Mary.

754.

Catharine[5] Glatfelter (John[4], &c.), m. J. Hamilton Joseph,
farm. N. Salem. Ch.: Albert, Hamilton, Edna, Lizzie,
Henry, Mary, Aden, Neada.

755.

HENRY[4] K. GLATFELTER, d. (Daniel[3], Henry[2], &c.), m.
1st, Louisa Erhart. Ch.: (756) James B. and Agnes,
1864; m. 2d, Sarah Mummert, now living at York, Pa.
Ch.: Raymond C., 1876, and Bessie, 1878.

756.

James[5] B. Gladfelter (Henry[4] K., Daniel[3], &c.), m. Lizzie
McLane. Res. Columbia, Pa. Railroading. Luth. Ch.:
Melvin I., 1876; Maud A., 1880; Miles H., 1885;
Mabel, 1885; Benard N., 1890; Edward, 1893; Guy J.,
1895, d.

757.

SARAH[4] A. GLATFELTER (Daniel[3], &c.), m. Israel Folcomer, N. Cordorus twp. Ch.: 2: (758) Jacob, m.

Ellen Holtzapple. Res. Baltimore, Md. Ch.: one; (759) Lillie, m. Lewis Falkenstine, N. Cod. twp. Ch.: 0.

760.

MELVINA[4] GLATFELTER (Daniel[3], &c.), m. Israel Eyster, N. Cod. twp. Ch.: 8: Henry. unm.; (761) Jacob, m. Hattie Kehr. Ch.: Peter; (762) Daniel; (763) Kate, m. Paul Strickhauser, York, Pa. Ch.: 0; (764) Sarah, m. James Folcomer. Ch.: 4; Maggie, unm.; Peter, d.; Ellen, d.

762.

Daniel[5] Eyster (Melvina[4], Daniel[3], &c.), m. Agnes Christ. Res. N. Salem, Pa. Ch.: Charles, Paul, Ada, Ralph, Clara, Esther, Sue, Earl.

765.

DANIEL[4] GLATFELTER, d. (Daniel[3], &c.), m. Anna Wiest. Res. W. Manchester twp. Ch.: 4: Daniel[5] S., unm., Cincinnati, Ohio; (766) Agnes[5] A., m. Harvey E. Sprenkle, Bair Sta., Pa. Ref. Ch.: Florence M., 1895; 2 children[5], d.

Chapter 21st.— HARRY.

767.

HARRY[3] GLATFELTER (Henry[2], Casper[1]), m. Kate Krout. Farm. Luth., buried at Wolf's church. Ch.: (768) Daniel; (772) John; (786) Adam, Aug. 22, 1818; Jacob; (795) Catharine; (796) Eva, m. Mr. Miller; (797) Nancy.

768.

DANIEL[4] GLATFELTER (Harry[3], Henry[2], &c.). Ch.: 3; (769) Daniel[5], m. Amanda Boblitz. Farm. at Okete.

Ch.: 4 sons and 3 daughters; (770) Henry[5], d., m. Jane
Lau. Res. at N. Salem, Pa. Ch.: (771) Nettie[6], m.
Alexander Baker, N. Salem. Ch.: William,[7] d.; George[5].

772.

JOHN[4] GLATFELTER (Harry[3], &c.) Res. near Okete, Pa.,
met death by accident on the railroad. Ch.: 13: (773)
Nathaniel[5] F., 1858; (774) Isaac[5] C.; (775) Annie[5], 1856,
m. Mr. Hibner. Ch.: 2, d.; (776) Ellen[5], 1856; (777)
Leah[5], m. Geo. Grim, Abbottstown, Pa. Ch.: 3; (778)
Charles[5] W., m. to un. Ch.: 0; Cornelius[5], 1866 unm.;
(779) Martha[5], 1865, m. Mr. Densler. Ch.: all dead;
(780) John[5]; (782) Henry[5], 1861–1889; (783) Bertha[5],
m. Mr. Road, Kirkwood, N. Jersey. Ch.: One. (784)
Christiana[5]; (785) Nettie[5], m. Mr. Klinedinst, York, Pa.

773.

Nathaniel[5] F. Gladfelter (John[4], Harry[3], &c.), m. Mary C.
Ernst. Lab. York, Pa. Pref. Luth. Wife, U. B.
Ch.: Lillie E., 1883; Emily M., 1885; Mary A., 1887;
Bessie, 1889; Myrtle D., 1891; Franklin C., 1894; Flora
V., 1895; Helen B., 1896; Anna M., 1898; John J.,
1900.

774.

Isaac[5] C. Glatfelter (John[4], &c.), m. Elizabeth Shrepple.
Mason. Res. York, Pa. Unaf. Wife a Meth. Ch.:
Rosie E., 1879; Frederick, 1882; Eugene, 1886; Elmer,
1892; Fannie, 1893; Margarete, 1899.

776.

Ellen[5] Gladfelter (John[4], &c.), m. Aaron B. Mickley (d.).
Widow, res. York, Pa. Pref. Ref. Ch.: Harry, 1882;
Alverda, 1887; Charles, 1888; Annie, 1891; Edna, 1893;
Nettie A., 1896.

780.

John[5] Gladfelter (John[4], &c.), m. Mary Swarts. Res. Sevenvalley. Lab. Ch.: H. Robert, 1875; (781) William

7

F., 1878, m. Jestie Reaver. Ch.: 0; Allen E., 1880; Charles E., 1883.

782.

Henry[5] Gladfelter, d. (John[4], &c.), m. Margaret Kendig. Widow, res. York, Pa. Luth. Ch.: Anna, 1883; Mary, 1884–1884; Ralph, 1885; Harry, 1887–1887; Roy, 1888–1891.

784.

Christiana[5] Gladfelter (John[4], &c.), m. Levi Bupp, teamster. York, Pa. Luth. Ch.: Edward L., 1881; Adam, 1884; Sarah, 1885; Nettie, 1893.

786.

ADAM[4] GLADFELTER (Harry[3], Henry[2], &c.), m. Elizabeth Ilgenfritz, d. Retired farm., res. York, Pa. Luth. Ch.: (787) Sarah, 1842; (789) Peter, 1845, m. 2d, Miss A. Zeigler; (790) Catharine, 1847; (791) Alexander, 1850; Leander, 1853; Eli, 1858, very recently, accidentally killed.

787.

Sarah[5] Glatfelter (Adam[4], Harry[3], &c.), m. Samuel Glassmeyer, lab., York, Pa. Moravian. Ch.: Rosie, 1861; (788) Harry, 1869, m. Tillie Lark. Ch.: Elsie May, 1890.

790.

Catharine[5] Glatfelter (Adam[4], &c.), m. E. T. Lewis, bricklayer, York, Pa. Meth. Ch.: Ida E., 1872; Marietta, Pa.; Priscilla A., 1880; Edward T., 1882; John A., 1885.

791.

Alexander[5] Glatfelter (Adam[4], &c.), m. Fannie E. Gotwalt. Carpenter, York, Pa. Ch.: (792) Minnie[6] E., 1871, m. Wm. E. Strine, Merch., York, Pa.; (793) Nettie[6] V., 1874, m. James R. Ness, York, Pa. Ch.: Gilmore, 1892, and Manola, 1895; (794) Clarence[6] A. (1876)

m. Florence G. Small. Carp. York, Pa. Unaf. Ch.: Clarence A., Wilbert, Naomi, Vina; Stewart[6] W., 1881; Kerwin[6] E., 1883; Norman[6] G., 1885; Fannie[6] E., 1888.

795.

CATHARINE[4] GLATFELTER (Harry[3], Henry[2], &c.), m. Eli Meyers, York, Pa. Milling (retired). Luth. Ch.: J. P., Oct., 1850; York, Pa., and Catharine, d. young.

797.

NANCY[4] GLATFELTER (Harry[3], Henry[2], &c.), m. 1st. Martin Emig. Ch.: Geo. F., 1853, d.; Catharine E., 1856; Martin P., 1859; Rosie A., 1862, d.; Henry E., 1864, d.; m. 2d, William Bowers, carp., York, Pa. U. B. Ch.: William H., 1869; Sarah A., 1870, d.; Charles E., 1872; (798) Ida J., 1867.

798.

Ida[5] J. Bowers (Nancy[4], Harry[3], &c.), m. Charles Smith, lab. York, Pa. Pref. U. B. Ch.: (799) Daisie I., 1883; m. Mr. Crosbly; Emma K., 1884; Mary E., 1885; George W., 1887; Minnie A., 1889; Harry E., 1898; Myrtle and Viola, 1893.

PERSONS REPORTED BUT NOT FOUND.

D. H. Gladfelter, Cleveland, Ohio.
Reuben F. Gladfelter, Cincinnati, Ohio.
Absalom Glatfelter, Columbia Grove, Iowa.
Harry J. Glatfelter, son of Daniel.

L. of C.

ADDENDA.

181a. John H. Stump, m. Emma J. Snyder. Ch.: Emma M., 1891–1897; Samuel W., 1894–1897; Ida M., 1897; Flora E., 1899.

199a. Chas. H. Keesey, 1847–1894, m. Elizabeth C. Hovis, Dallastown, Pa. Ch.: Percy E., 1870; Minnie M., 1873.

446. Add, Mary A., 1854–1863; Allen, 1860; Anna M., 1870–1877; Sallie S., 1874–1875.

448. Add, Paul F., 1884.

451. Substitute Harry E., 1890; George L., 1892.

NOTE A.— THE LIVING OF THE FOURTH GENERATION.

The following list includes all those known of by the author and is probably complete or nearly so : —

William, Jonathan, and Charles Folckommer, of Margaretta, of Felix.
Margaretta, (m. Lowe) of Margaretta, of Felix.
Elizabeth, (m. Wagner) of Philip, of Felix.
Israel, 70 years old, Ohio, of Daniel, of Felix.
Granville, b. 1836; Brillhart's Sta., Pa., of Frederick, of Felix.
Anna M., b. 1841; (m. Fahs) York, Pa., of Frederick, of Felix.
Daniel J., b. 1820; York, Pa., of John, of Felix.
Jesse Hovis, b. 1823; Spry, York co., Pa., of Barbara, of Felix.
Franklin Hovis, b. 1827, York, Pa., of Barbara, of Felix.

John, b. 1827; New Salem, Pa., of Daniel, of Henry.
Eliza, b. 1822, (m. Fishel) New Salem, Pa., of Daniel, of Henry.
Rebecca, b. 1820, (m. Miller) York co., Pa., of Daniel, of Henry.
Jacob B., b. 1836; Okete, Pa., of Jacob, of Henry.
Andrew, b. 1837; Okete, Pa., of Jacob, of Henry.
David B., b. 1832; Brillhart Sta., Pa., of Jacob, of Henry.
Louisa, unm.; York, Pa., of Jacob, of Henry.
Adam, b. 1820; York, Pa., of Harry, of Henry.
Nancy, (m. Bowers) York, Pa., of Harry, of Henry.
Ephraim, b. 1836; Okete, Pa., of Michael, of Henry and his three sisters, Caroline, Sarah, Matilda (probably).

Ferre, Israel, b. 1828; Hellam P. O., Pa., of Rosanna, of John.
Forscht, Israel, b. 1838; York, Pa., of Susan, of John.
Forscht, Elizabeth, b. 1831, (m. Miller) Savannah, Ga., of Susan, of John.
Elizabeth, b. 1831, (m. Lentz) York, Pa., of George, of John.

Casper, Havana, Kansas, of Casper, of Casper.
Frederick, b. 1844; Princeville, Ill., of Casper, of Casper.
Jacob, b. 1831; York, Pa., of Casper, of Casper.
Susan, b. 1840, m. Tarbox; Princeville, Ill., of Casper, of Casper.

NOTE B. — EIGHTH GENERATION.

It will be noticed that nearly all the living belong to the fifth, sixth, and seventh generations. Those of the fourth are listed in Note A. above. Those of the eighth — the vanguard — are the following: —

Walter[8] C. Kauffman, b. March 15th, 1894; Abraham[8] F. Kauff., Sept. 28, 1899, of Harvey[7] C. Kauffman (Salina[6], Franklin[5], Jacob[4], John[3], Felix[2]).

Esther[6] M. Lerew, b. 1896; inft. b. 1898; Roy C., b. 1900, — children of Martha[7] Day, of Henry[6] Day, of Lucinda[5] Keesey, of Elizabeth[4] Glatfelter, of Jacob[3], John[2], Casper[1].

Mocleta Reever, b. 1897; Cora E. Reever, 1898; Kerwin H. Rever, 1900, — children of Leah Day, sister of the preceding.

A child[8] of Mr. Emig m. Sarah[7] Hoke, of Wm.[6] J. Glatfelter, of Jacob[5], Charles[4], Philip[3], Felix[2], Casper.[1]

Annie[6] E. Keach, b. 1900 (Clara[7] Small, Ella[6] S. Glatfelter, Amos[5], Jacob[4], Jacob[3], John[2], Casper[1]).

NOTE C. — KINSHIP.

It will be noticed that all of the third generation were first cousins; those of the fourth are second cousins; all of the fifth, third cousins; and so on. Thus comparing any generation of any one of the four branches with the same generation of any other branch the relationship is readily perceived.

NOTE D. — INCREASE.

My record is far from being complete, yet it embraces 861 families containing 3,065 descendants from the one ancestor, Casper.

From a scientific standpoint, an entirely complete record of such a rapidly multiplying family as the one exhibited in this book, would be very interesting.

The record as it is represented here, including only the four branches, viz.: of John, Felix, Casper, and Henry, shows the following succession of increases: Gen. 1st, 1; 2d, 4; 3d, 33; 4th, 176; 5th, 749; 6th, 1,319, — the last three not being complete. The descendants of three of the 3d gen., viz., of Jacob³, Felix²; of Philip³, Henry²; of Rosanna³, Casper², being missing.

The dates of the beginning of the successive generations, after the second, are as follows: the 3d, 1778 (about); 4th, 1800 (about); 5th, 1824; 6th, 1848; 7th, 1870; 8th, 1894, showing a new generation to have stepped forth at each period of 22 or 24 years.

NOTE E.

Too late for the body of this work were received baptismal and marriage records of the Glattfelders at the church of Glattfelden, carefully investigated by the Rev. Edwin Jaggli, its present pastor, and communicated to S. F. Glatfelter, Esq., York, Pa. The earliest record is 1674, the birth of Felix, father of our Casper. Records antecedent are said to be lost, " though it is certain the name of Glattfelder dates very far back." " Felix' father Hans was a Deacon of the church." " Glattfelders held important offices in the town. One was *Ammann* (President and Sheriff), and Hans, the brother of Felix, was Judge in the 17th century. Later, another, was again *Ammann*." " There are now three Glattfelder families living at Glattfelden. The forefathers of this name were of the Reformed faith (Zwingli)." For the information of our Glotfelty friends, the record of their ancestral immigrant, Solomon, is given as the son of Casper, born Feb. 23d, 1738,— precisely the date given me by Mr. Josiah M. Glotfelty, Lanark, Ill.

INDEX OF THE GLATFELTER NAMES.

INDEX OF NAMES OTHER THAN GLATFELTER.

www.ingramcontent.com/pod-product-compliance
Lightning Source LLC
Chambersburg PA
CBHW031532260326
41914CB00026B/1658